Yeshivath Beth Moshe of Scranton
is proud of its many contributions
to Torah Scholarship.
Since its beginning in 1965,
the Scranton Yeshiva has elevated
the calibre of Torah education
throughout its high school, *beis medrash*,
and Kollel-Graduate Program.
Our alumni rank
among the leading Torah educators
and lay leaders in America.

Over the years, dissemination of
valuable, informative and spiritually uplifting
Jewish literature
has become a tradition at
Yeshivath Beth Moshe.
It is in this tradition
that we present with pride
this currrent volume.

DESTINY

THE STORY OF THE
JEWISH PEOPLE
AND THE WESTERN WORLD

DESTINY

THE STORY OF THE JEWISH PEOPLE AND THE WESTERN WORLD

VOLUME ONE

FROM THE BIRTH OF THE PATRIARCHS TO
THE BEGINNING OF THE SECOND TEMPLE ERA

Yaakov Yosef Reinman

ISBN 0-962-6226-5-6

Published in conjuction with
Yeshivath Beth Moshe, Scranton, PA.

Book and cover design by Deenee Cohen.
Cartography and typography by Chaya Bleier.

This volume is part of a larger work-in-progress.
The author would very much appreciate the
comments, criticism and suggestions of readers.
Please address all correspondence to the author
care of the publisher:

Olive Tree Press
674 Eighth Street
Lakewood, NJ 08701

לזכר נשמת
אמי מורתי
יענטא בת ר' חיים אייזיק ע"ה
ת. נ. צ. ב. ה.

*This book is dedicated to
the memory of
my mother,
who taught me the value of knowledge.*

Table of Contents

Preface

F ive years ago, I undertook the rather limited project of writing an essay on the historical roots of the holocaust from an Orthodox Jewish perspective. At the time, I knew I would have to concentrate on the seminal events of the nineteenth century in the wake of Napoleon's conquests, such as the formation of a distinctive Germanic culture and the assimilationist trends among the newly emancipated Jews. But as I tried to describe the developments of the last century, I found it necessary to go back even further to examine their own roots in earlier times.

Slowly but inexorably, I found my investigation broadening and deepening as I was drawn farther and farther back into the billowing mists of time. Finally, I found myself standing in the Mesopotamia of four thousand years ago, looking ahead at an intellectual journey that would take me through the entire political and philosophical history of the Western world. I was overwhelmed, but there was no turning back.

This book is the result of that intellectual journey. The chapters I have devoted to the holocaust are longer than the essay I had originally intended to write, but they are not the focus of this study. Rather, I have focused on identifying and tracing, from a strictly Jewish ideological viewpoint, the underlying forces of destiny that have governed the last four millennia of history and will most probably continue to direct the fortunes of mankind for the foreseeable future. The holocaust may have been an aberration in its inhuman savagery, but at least with hindsight, we can identify it as only one of the many periodic explosions that fit neatly into the tortured pattern of Western civilization.

The opinions and interpretations presented in the following pages are deeply rooted in traditional rabbinic scholarship and the ardent beliefs of the core element of the Jewish people. The credentials I bring to this undertaking are an intimate knowledge of my own people and faith, a lifelong interest in world history and a background in Talmudic scholarship; the analytical and interpretive style is largely the product of the Talmudic method I have absorbed during my many years of study.

In some ways, this book is a work of history, but in others, it is really a work of philosophy. I have not approached my subject as an allegedly objective historian who brings to his task a clean slate on which his prejudices and preconceptions are inscribed in invisible ink. Rather, I have come with a full baggage of religious and philosophical beliefs, and through these beliefs, I have attempted to give meaning to the patterns of history.

According to the teachings of Judaism, the entire world was created as a setting for the achievement of the perfect union between man and God, and all of history is the result of the interplay between divine providence and human choice. Jewish history is, therefore, not a self-contained drama that takes place in a corner of the larger arena of world events. Rather, Jewish history examines the entire world from a specifically Jewish perspective which puts the Jewish people and their destiny squarely in the center of universal history. Consequently, this book attempts to present an integrated history of the world, with particular emphasis on the history of the Jewish people and the historical development of the Torah.

Unfortunately, however, the Jewish people have become ideologically fragmented, especially during recent centuries, and a number of viewpoints now claim to represent the Jewish perspective. Still, only one viewpoint has been maintained by the core element of the Jewish people, without interruption, for the entire three-thousand-year span of Jewish national history. After every period of fragmentation in Jewish history, this same core element has emerged to carry the banner of Judaism into the future. Even the most casual sampling of Jewish literature throughout its historical development immediately yields the salient feature of the core Jewish ideology—a belief in the divine origin and the immutability of the Written and Oral Torah. All schismatic movements that deviated from this central tenet eventually faded away.

In our own times, this core ideology has been labeled Orthodox Judaism, a general classification which encompasses numerous shadings and divisions, all of which regard the Torah as the ultimate source of truth, wisdom and human guidance. This viewpoint, which has endured with continuity and longevity throughout Jewish history, does not incorporate essential elements and attitudes of other cultures and, as such, can be considered exclusively Jewish. This is the viewpoint to which I subscribe and the vantage point from which I have approached my work.

This book, therefore, differs from most other English-language Jewish histories in the sense that it lends more credence to the venerated Books of the Prophets than to the gossip of Herodotus; that it interprets the Scriptures according to rabbinic literature composed by Torah sages and not according to the distortions of gentile Bible critics virtually ignorant of the language and method of the Torah; that it recognizes the Talmud as a work of unsurpassed genius and infinite depth whose surface has barely been scratched by two thousand years of intense scholarly study; that it discerns a direct link between the religious imperatives of Judaism and the historical destiny of the Jewish people; that it views all developments of world events within the context of the historical progress of the Jewish ideal.

The particular viewpoint of this book is also reflected in the identification of historical eras for the last four thousand years of history. The nine historical periods—the Ages of Formation, Confrontation, Dispersion, Oppression, Persecution, Emancipation, Incubation, Explosion and Rejuvenation—are differentiated by the more fundamental shifts in the relationship between the Jewish people and the world at large. (This special preview edition covers only the Age of Formation.)

The treatment of each of these periods is, of necessity, compressed and thematic. In general, I have tried to avoid the thickets of minutiae through which historians often wander; some arcane materials have been relegated to the Notes, while others have been omitted altogether. The informed reader will, of course, have a greater appreciation for the development of the themes, but prior familiarity with history is not necessary for a reading of this book.

For the early periods, which rely heavily on Biblical and Talmudic sources, I have tried to include only essentially historical material; the amount of space devoted to certain personages and events as opposed to others does not reflect on their relative greatness or religious impact but on their historical significance.

The primary sources for the narrative covering the Biblical period are, of course, the First Books of the Prophets—*Joshua, Judges, Samuel* and *Kings*. The narrative has been augmented, however, by supplementary material which appears in the parallel accounts of *Chronicles, Jeremiah* and some of the other Latter Books of the Prophets or Hagiographa. The authority for any inference not readily apparent from a simple reading of the text is given in the Notes and Sources.

Furthermore, the Bible and Talmud abound with opaque passages that are indecipherable without the rabbinic glosses and commentaries. These sources have been cited from time to time in the Notes, but the reader must be aware that, for the most part, they are not available in translation, only in Hebrew or in the Hebrew-Aramaic Talmudic dialect.

With regards to world history, the basic data presented in the following pages are to be found in any collegiate level survey text, but the interpretations certainly are not. Much of the more detailed factual information derives from the extensive research of Will and Ariel Durant in *The Story of Civilization,* which I have accepted at face value without going back to check all the original sources. The sources for other information have been indicated.

With regards to dates in the pre-Alexandrian period, I have followed the Jewish system, which differs significantly from the secular system. In the Jewish system, the Persian Empire lasted half a century; thus, the destruction of the First Temple by the Babylonians, who preceded the Persians, is set in 423 b.c.e. However, Greek history from the Persian War until Alexander's conquest of Persia seems to stretch for two centuries, and thus, the destruction of the Temple is placed in 586 b.c.e. But if so, we are left with two "lost centuries" of Jewish history for which, incredibly, no records exist. In a lengthy article in a prestigious Israeli publication, based on a work in progress, Dr. Chaim Chaifetz offers a solution to this enigma. He suggests that much recorded Persian history actually took place under the Babylonian aegis before the Persian accession to imperial power and that the Jewish dates are indeed accurate.

For the transliteration of most Hebrew names and terms, I have used the inexact but familiar Anglicized forms, but for words less likely to be known to the general reader, I have reverted to the exact, phonetic transliteration, according to the Ashkenazic pronunciations.

In closing, I would like to express my appreciation and gratitude to all the people who have assisted and supported me throughout this difficult project. I would like to extend a special note of acknowledgment to my good friends Rabbi Yaakov Schnaidman, Rabbi Chaim Bressler and Rabbi Shmuel Flam of Yeshivah Beth Moshe of Scranton, Pennsylvania, for their close involvement in this project from its very inception; their participation in this special edition is indeed an honor and a privilege. I would also like to take this opportunity to thank them for the warmth and attention they have lavished on my son Berel, whom I have entrusted into their capable hands, and for instilling in him a love for Torah scholarship and our hallowed Jewish ideals. May God grant them long life, good health and the strength to continue their important work for many years to come.

I would like to give special thanks to my good friend Shmuel Kessner, Professor of History, the Graduate School of the City University of New York, for his close reading of the manuscript and his numerous comments and corrections. I would also like to thank: my esteemed colleague in the publishing field Mrs. Raizy Kaufman, for her critical review and insightful suggestions; Mrs. Deenee Cohen, for her elegant cover and interior design; Mrs. Chaya Bleier, for her professional typography and cartography. In particular, I would like to express my profound appreciation for the patience, expertise and support, both technical and moral, of my wife Shami, who skillfully guided the manuscript through its earlier stages. My God grant us all the ability and the opportunity to serve Him in health and happiness and to bring honor to His name amd enlightenment to His people.

Y. Y. R.
Rosh Chodosh Adar Rishon 5755 (1995)
Lakewood, New Jersey

prologue

The Search for Destiny

The first question about history that occurs to a believer in God in search of destiny is: Can the conscious actions of men change the course of events or is everything preordained by divine plan?

According to the teachings of Judaism, the ultimate result of history is preordained, but the intervening process and the length of its duration are in the hands of mankind. Ultimately, history will arrive at a messianic age when "swords will be beaten into plowshares"[1] and "the world will be filled with knowledge,"[2] when all the filters of evil will be removed and the unfettered light of the Divine Presence will penetrate to the darkest corners of the earth. But how will that point be reached? That is in the hands of mankind.

If mankind succeeds in overcoming the base instincts of the human condition and rising to the highest levels of goodness and spirituality, the messianic age will be ushered in through merit. If, on the other hand, mankind becomes so debased and degenerate that there is no longer any reasonable hope of improvement, the messianic age will be ushered in through necessity. But as long as mankind is caught somewhere in the middle between total good and total evil,[3] as long as there is hope for the voluntary achievement of the human ideal and a

17

meritorious entry into the messianic age, the painful process of history will drag on.

Man has been given the gift of choice. He has the free will to choose between good and evil, and he is rewarded or punished according to his choices. God already knows when the messianic age will come about and how it will be ushered in, but in the meantime, the determination of these questions is in the hands of mankind.

History, then, is the chronicle of choices. World history is the chronicle of national choices, the collective choices of entire groups and societies. National history is the chronicle of individual choices within those groups and societies. The individual choices determine the collective choice of the group, and then the collective choices interact with each other to affect the course of world history.

In the following pages, we will attempt to trace the tapestry of collective choices that have brought the world to its present condition. At the same time, we will try to identify and evaluate the individual choices within the Jewish nation that have determined its internal condition as it was buffeted along the perilous course of world events.

As we look at history in an attempt to discover the complex recipe of forces that brought the world to its present state, we are first struck by spectacles of chaos and confusion. The landscape changes constantly over the short span of a few thousand years. Civilizations rise and fall. Empires appear, spread out and fade away. Ideologies and systems are born, tested and discarded. Cities are built and destroyed by endless wars. Technology and communications forge ahead, continuously accelerating the pace of change, compressing centuries into decades, years or even days. Generation after generation battles for a hold on the present and yearns for a future that never seems to arrive. What is it all about? What drives man to spend his fleeting moment of life on this earth in violent struggles and mad pursuits?

If we look closely, however, we can discern a certain method to the madness. We can discern the faint outlines of threads that wind their way through the clutter and rubble of history. These threads represent the road to the future, to the ultimate fate of mankind. They are the forces of our destiny.

The forces of destiny inhabit the world of ideas, of striving, of beliefs. Like people, they combine and reproduce, and their offspring combine and reproduce again. A person is never identical to his ancestors, yet he is bonded to them by the very fibers of his being. In the same way, the forces of destiny are very different from their predecessors, but also very much the same.

But where must we look for these threads? The world is full of societies, each with its own history, religious beliefs and cultural imperatives, its own forces of destiny; are all of them central to the common destiny of mankind? Clearly not. If we are to consider the destiny of mankind as a whole, we must concentrate on those forces that have affected the history of mankind as a whole. These threads, the mainlines of history so to speak, are to be found in the determinant zone of world history, an area which can arguably be called the Imperial Quadrant.

Today, the Imperial Quadrant is a large geographic rectangle which is bounded on the east by the Ural Mountains, on the south by the Tropic of Cancer and on the west by the Pacific Ocean. The imperial military and economic power of the Quadrant controls the security and prosperity of mankind, and its ideas and culture permeate the farthest corners of the earth.

This is where the forces of world destiny are to be found. The Cold War between the United States and the Soviet Union, the two dominant powers of the Quadrant in the middle of the twentieth century, had a profound effect on the entire globe. The reverberations of the earlier wars between Germany and Britain, Britain and France, France and Spain were felt to the very ends of the earth. But the bloody war outside the Quadrant between India and Pakistan in 1971 did not threaten the security of our homes.

Japan, China and India, the three giants of East Asia, all stand alone. There has never been unity among them, nor is there ever likely to be, and individually, they are not a threat to the world at large. Even Japan, which has shown regional military power and global economic power, is not a significant geopolitical factor on its own. There is not much danger of a Japanese, Chinese or Indian military presence in Europe or

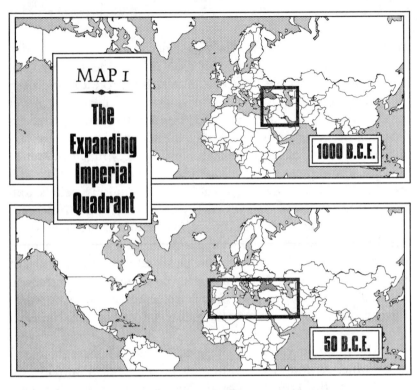

MAP I

The Expanding Imperial Quadrant

1000 B.C.E.

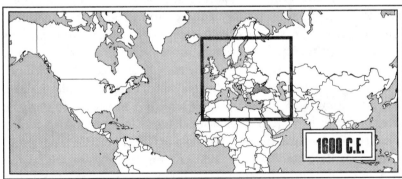

50 B.C.E.

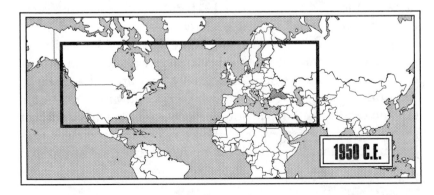

1600 C.E.

1950 C.E.

North America, but all of these countries have been occupied at one time or another by a power from the Quadrant.

Further afield, Southern Asia, Southern Africa and Latin America have never possessed global powers. Australia, Indonesia, South Africa, Nigeria, Brazil and the like are important members of the international community but not potential shakers of the world.

The internal histories of all these nations are therefore not critical to overall world destiny, because whatever social and political form they take is not likely to upset the equilibrium of the rest of the world. Only in alliance with a power from the Quadrant do they take on global significance, and therefore, their experiences affect world destiny only if they influence the Quadrant. Otherwise, they are of practical interest only to their regional neighbors.

An understanding of the last thousand years of Indian history may be politically important for Bangladesh and Pakistan but not for the rest of the world. An understanding of the last thousand years of Germanic or Slavic history, however, will give us a glimpse into the future of world history. Therefore, we must seek the keys to the destiny of mankind in the Imperial Quadrant. The history of the West is the history of the world.

As we go back into history, the Imperial Quadrant shrinks. One hundred years ago, it was bounded on the west by the Atlantic rather than the Pacific. Two thousand years ago, it was bounded on the north by the Alps. Three thousand years ago, it was bounded on the west by the Nile River and on the north by Asia Minor. At this point, before the shift of power to Europe, the Quadrant included only Western Asia and the northeastern tip of Africa, but the civilization, the ideas and the religions of Europe all originated in the ancient Quadrant. The thoughts and feelings of the Quadrant through every stage of its expansion live on today in one form or another. Therefore, we must look carefully at the last three thousand years of history in the Quadrant if we are to gain even the slightest insight into our common destiny.

It is the thesis of this book that the underlying thread of Western history is the ideological conflict that arose in the Quadrant between the Jewish world view and the Greek world view. Human society cannot exist without a deity, an object of communal worship that serves as the fountainhead of aspirations and ideals. In the Jewish view, that deity is God. In the Greek view, that deity is Man. The unresolved struggle for dominion of the world, whether it will become a Kingdom of God or a Kingdom of Man, is the engine that drives world history. The Jewish and the Greek positions are at the two opposite poles of Western civilization, and all major ideologies and movements in the Western world fall somewhere into the magnetic field between these two poles.

As we follow the progress of history, we see the spread of the Judeo-Greek ideological conflict across the centuries and millennia of Western history. We see it adapt repeatedly to changing social, political, technological and geographical conditions. We see it play a crucial role in the rise and fall of the Roman Empire, the emergence of Christianity and Islam, the feudal Germanic kingdoms, the Renaissance, the Enlightenment, the Scientific Revolution and the birth of secular humanism, fascism and socialism in the modern era.

We cannot fully understand the Judeo-Greek conflict, however, unless we go back to their formative periods in ancient times. In the centuries of their youth, both the Jewish and Greek civilizations strove to create higher cultures that would elevate mankind; both sought a state of expanded spirit and mind that totally transcended the purely physical condition. But these two cultures were so different from each other that when they met it immediately became clear that one would ultimately have to destroy the other. The ensuing life-and-death struggle is the history of the world.

PART I

The Age of Formation

And Abraham prostrated himself, and the Lord spoke with him, saying, "Behold, I am making a covenant with you, and you shall be the father of a multitude of nations. . . And I will uphold my covenant between Myself and you and your descendants as an everlasting covenant to you and to your descendants."

(Genesis 17:3-7)

I

Modern Times

*All that exists has already existed, and
all that happens has already happened,
for there is nothing new under the sun.*
(Ecclesiastes 1:9)

People tend to think of their own times as the modern era and of earlier times as medieval or ancient. Looking around at the world of our own generation, we see the phenomenal advances in science, technology, transportation, communications and the visual arts, and we think that surely our times are the most advanced and enlightened in history. Surely, we tell ourselves, the social ills that still plague us are just baggage from earlier times, baggage soon to be discarded forever. Earlier times, in our perception, are blanketed in a haze of a certain darkness because they did not know what we know now, and we look upon them with a measure of condescension. "Those were the olden days," we say. "But these are modern times."

But let us for a moment imagine a future historian's view of our own times. For example, it is conceivable that someday historians will describe our times as the Socialist Century, the century of paternalistic societies, from the outright communist

countries to the capitalist democracies with intrusive social bu-
reaucracies. It is quite conceivable that these future historians
will study the collapse of the failed systems and compare them
unfavorably with the more advanced forms of government and
society of their own times. And we can easily imagine them
shaking their heads at the befuddlement that must have blanketed the world in the twentieth century. Yet we who are living
at the turn of the twenty-first century still look back at the past
hundred years as "the modern times." All times are modern
when they transpire.

Three thousand years ago, when the shining light of Judaism first came into existence, the world was a very modern
place. The Imperial Quadrant,[1] the focal point of world history
that would eventually project its power and influence to every
corner of the earth, was still confined to the eastern rim of the
Mediterranean basin, but great things were happening there.
Major imperial systems had arisen in the Quadrant and were
effecting profound changes in the way people lived and
thought.

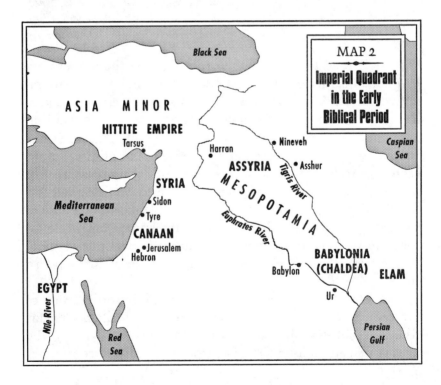

MAP 2

Imperial Quadrant in the Early Biblical Period

On the northeastern tip of Africa, the ancient kingdom of Egypt flourished in the splendid isolation of the Nile River valley, protected on all sides by sea and desert, while in the Mesopotamian region of Western Asia, in the lush valleys of the Tigris and Euphrates Rivers, many diverse and powerful nationalities battled each other for supremacy.

In a pattern formed over the centuries, one nation would conquer the river valleys of Mesopotamia and establish an empire. Having to contend with predatory neighbors on all sides, the empire would inevitably fall victim to invasion and conquest. A new empire would be established, and the cycle would begin again. In this fashion, we witness the succession to imperial power of Sumerians, Akkadians, Amorites, Babylonians, Assyrians, Chaldeans, Medes and Persians amidst constantly expanding imperial borders which ultimately extended into Egypt and to the western shores of the Black Sea.[2]

Yet for all the warfare and conquests, the civilization that emerged in this arena was relatively stable. The empires that succeeded each other retained the same basic political, economic, social and cultural structures. Notable cities, such as Ur, Nineveh and Babylon, rose on the banks of the fabled rivers, and although their masters may have changed from time to time, the cities continued to grow and prosper.[3] Immense irrigation systems crisscrossed the valleys, expanding the boundaries of the Fertile Crescent and increasing the bounties that poured forth from the well-slaked soil and found their way, in one form or another, into the treasurehouses of the cities.

The cities themselves were the focal points of society, places where the heartbeat of cultural vitality throbbed and pulsated, where even a person from our own times might have savored many of the comforts enjoyed by the privileged classes. Magnificent temples dominated the high points of the cities. Splendid palaces lined the thoroughfares and avenues, and a latticework of streets and alleyways teemed with the masses of the commonfolk. People of every size, color and attire, speaking a cacophony of languages, crowded into the marketplaces to inspect livestock, produce, spices, textiles, jewelry, pottery, tools and all manner of condiments, implements and adornments transported from storied places in faraway lands.

Legal systems protected people from the whims of tyrants and attempted to provide impartial justice for all. Education and knowledge grew slowly but steadily, with advanced discoveries in geography, astronomy, calendar keeping, mathematics, engineering and medicine. The science and art of warfare surged ahead; huge armies, equipped with chariots and siege machines, were led by generals schooled in tactics and strategy.

The ancient imperial governments were highly sophisticated as well, employing thousands in the diplomatic corps and military administration, the offices of taxation and finance, the judicial system and the regulation of commerce. Skilled scribes recorded the chronicles of kings and wars and all the other business of government, leaving written evidence of a vibrant world that, except for technological differences, was not so dissimilar to our own.

In the concept of religion, however, the ancient world differed dramatically from our own. The ancients were acutely aware of their own mortal limitations. The control of the forces of nature and the vicissitudes of fortune were clearly in other hands—in the hands of the gods. But what was a god to the ancient mind, and what was the relationship of ancient man to his gods?

Let us suppose for a moment that a race of aliens, immeasurably more intelligent and powerful than human beings, has invaded the earth in our own times. Let us suppose that these aliens control the entire world, that they are so powerful that it would be foolish to resist, just as it would be totally futile for an animal species to rise up against the human race. In such an eventuality, it would be only wise for the human race to reach an accommodation with the new reality, to do anything to placate and appease the alien conquerors. But after such an accommodation, things could never go back to the way they were. The human race would no longer stand at the pinnacle of creation. Henceforth, it would be demoted to a servile role, a talented but inferior species at the mercy of its alien masters.

Such was the ancient concept of the gods. According to the understanding of the ancients, the world was populated by numerous powerful, capricious and unseen creatures who controlled the destiny and fortunes of mankind, creatures who were spiritual only in the sense that they were invisible and immortal but who were material in every other sense. At their whim, these creatures could provide bountiful rains or bring famine and pestilence. They could strike a man dead or give him riches and success. They could look down benignly on human affairs or they could vent their anger with thunder, lightning and fiery storms.

Over the millennia, men came to identify and give names to these imaginary masters, the race of the gods. Mythological legends described the lives of these gods, their marriages and familial relationships and their struggles with other gods. Men paid homage and brought sacrifices to the gods in temples erected in their honor, in the fervent hope that the gods would be appeased and would not bring misery and sorrow to mankind.

The ancient pantheon of gods was, of course, not universal by any means. Different nations had their own sets of deities and myths, although they frequently borrowed from their neighbors. War and conquest also contributed greatly to the fortunes of the gods, with the gods of the victors being imposed on the vanquished and the gods of the vanquished often being adopted by the victors. And even when empires crumbled and conquerors were expelled from their fields of conquest, the gods they had brought with them often remained behind, at least in a subordinate role to the local gods. Religious tolerance was the order of the day; there was always room for another god.

Thus, the relationship with the gods became the most important feature of society. Incalculable wealth was lavished on the temples that housed the gods and the priestly classes. Idols representing the various gods appeared not only in the temples but in every household, and all aspects of human life were interwoven in a tapestry of superstitions. Governments represented the authority of the gods, and in Egypt, the pharaoh actually ruled by unquestioned whim because he was believed to be descended from the god race.

Yet for all their looming domination, the gods themselves were absorbed in their own lives and not much concerned with the human race. As long as they were properly appeased, the gods made no moral or ethical demands on men. They did not seem to care about good and evil and had only a passing interest in the proper administration of justice; they desired no particular code of conduct. The gods enjoyed the homage and sacrifices offered up by the inferior human race and then went about their own business; they were no better than men, just immeasurably stronger. Men did not enhance their inner selves by their contact with the gods, and any love they may have felt for the gods was the love of a dog for his master who has fed him and patted him on the head.

Relegated to the status of an inferior species, the people of the ancient world could not develop a sense of ultimate historical destiny or a philosophy that addressed the profound questions of human existence. Men were interlopers in the domain of the gods, thankful for a modicum of peace and a moment of pleasure in a life without higher purpose or goals. The ornaments of culture were merely for physical gratification. Literature recorded heroic exploits and popular myths and was devoid of ideals. Music was for merriment and diversion. Art was for the glorification of kings and the temples of the gods. Life was wanton and overburdened with layer upon layer of myth and superstition, a constant struggle to appease the capricious gods and curry their favor.

Within this purposeless hotbed of energy and superstition, there arose one of the greatest men in the history of the world, a man whose clarity of thought and purity of character would have an incredible impact on all future generations, whose ideas and actions would have a more meaningful effect on the destiny of mankind than all the empires and civilizations of his time. The man was Abraham, and his legacy to the world was Judaism.

2

---◆---

The Birth of Judaism

*And your offspring shall be a blessing to
all the nations of the earth, for you have
heeded My Voice.*

(Genesis 22:18)

Abraham was born in 1813 b.c.e. in Mesopotamia to the
wealthy House of Terah, an aristocratic family of Semitic
lineage. He spent his youth in the flourishing Chaldean
city of Ur in the lower Euphrates valley, a pampered son
destined for a life of luxury and privilege. As a member of the
highest stratum of Mesopotamian society, the choicest fruits of
civilization were his for the asking, but Abraham was, above all
else, a man of truth.

Unimpressed by the preconceived notions of the society in
which he lived, Abraham decided to take an honest look at the
world around him. With remarkable perspicacity and intellectual courage, he came to the realization that the prevalent
idolatrous cults did not provide satisfactory answers to the fundamental questions of existence and that the god race was, in
fact, a figment of human imagination. Instead, he discerned the
existence of a single, unknowable Deity who was the true Master
of the Universe.

According to Abraham's new insight, the world was created by a Supreme Being whose nature was beyond the realm of human understanding. Nevertheless, the virtually infinite complexity and variety of the universe were resounding testimony to the existence of a Master Designer.

Furthermore, since everything that existed had to be created, it stood to reason that the world was created *ex nihilo*, out of nothingness; the Creator had obviously brought everything into existence simply by willing it to be. Such unfathomable and boundless power could only belong to a Supreme Being completely beyond space and time, a single, limitless and totally spiritual Supreme Being. Such a Perfect Being, having no lacks or needs, must have created the world out of pure benevolence, and a person who obeyed the Will of the Creator was surely in the best position to receive the emanations of divine benevolence toward the human race. Through obedience, therefore, a person achieved exaltation rather than abject servility.

Abraham had discovered God, and by doing so, he had smashed the shackles of the god race and raised the status of the human race to unprecedented levels. Man was no longer an inferior creature struggling to survive in the shadow of the god race. He represented the highest form of life on the face of the earth, a glorious creature deeply imbued with the divine spirit. Man had a purpose in life and a destiny, and he stood at the pinnacle of creation.

For his great courage and clarity of vision, Abraham was rewarded with the gift of prophecy, and thenceforth, God communicated directly with Abraham from time to time. In the city of Ur, however, Abraham's new discovery was not greeted with enthusiasm but with dismay. Had Abraham simply suggested that the god race had only one member instead of many, it would have been revolutionary enough. But Abraham had introduced a totally new concept of divinity that undermined the foundations of Mesopotamian society. The power structure, the institutions and the rituals and customs were so completely associated with the idolatrous cults that to accept Abraham's view would have required dismantling society and rebuilding it anew. Moreover, it would bring an end to the promiscuous life style man had enjoyed under the indifferent gaze of the god race. Under the stern gaze of a moral God, man assumed a heavy mantle of responsibility along with his elevated state.

For a number of years, Abraham was harassed and persecuted in the city of Ur, until God directed him to uproot his entire household and set out for the distant land of Canaan on the Mediterranean coast. On the first leg of his journey, he reached the city of Harran near the border of Syria, where he remained for a long time. In Harran, far removed from the center of Mesopotamian imperial power, he publicized his views and gathered about him a sizable following. When he finally set out on the last leg of his journey to Canaan, many of his new followers joined him.

The Canaan that awaited Abraham was a slender strip of land alongside the Mediterranean Sea, a land of extraordinary beauty and great topographical variety, with mountain ranges, plateaus, rolling hills, coastal plains, broad valleys and deserts. Seven kindred Canaanite tribes lived in dozens of petty kingdoms sprinkled across the length and the breadth of the land. These tribes were the Canaanites, Hittites, Amorites, Hivites, Perizites, Jebusites and Girgashites.[1] Another important Canaanite people, the Phoenicians, lived in the Lebanese cities of Sidon and Tyre far to the north. Most of the people of

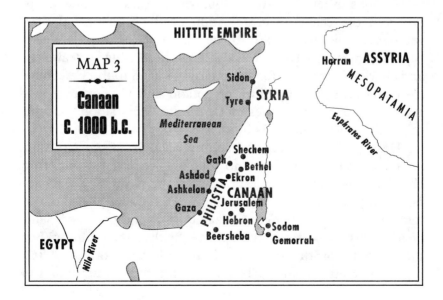

Canaan spoke Hebrew or some variation of it,[2] while the prevalent language of Mesopotamia was the related Aramaic.[3]

Canaan was a strategically important land sitting astride the major trade and invasion routes of the Near East. To the north, a branch of the Hittites had established an extensive empire that reached into Asia Minor. To the east, a different branch of the Amorites, under the leadership of the renowned King Hammurabi, held imperial power in Mesopotamia, with their capital in the great city of Babylon. To the south lay Egypt, the still feared but declining kingdom of the pharaohs. In the long shadow of their mighty neighbors, the people of Canaan barricaded themselves in the heavily fortified cities of their petty kingdoms, paying tribute and homage to their more powerful neighbors but clinging tenaciously to their own independence.[4]

Perhaps because of their political fragmentation and isolation, the peoples of Canaan developed a singularly self-centered and degenerate society. Although they paid tribute to their imperial neighbors, they did not themselves belong to any of the great empires, and therefore, their lives were centered around their own prosperous little kingdoms; they did not have the sense of social responsibility and transcendent aspirations usually found among citizens of large and powerful nations. They sought no glory, no cultural achievements, no spiritual satisfactions other than the jealous safeguarding of their property and the ceaseless gratification of their physical desires without the slightest regard for decency or propriety. The concepts of integrity in business dealings, hospitality to travellers and charitable concern for the poor were alien to the Canaanite mentality. The wealthy cities of Sodom and Gomorrah epitomized the extreme reaches of Canaanite degradation, but the other cities were not far behind.

Here, in the political and cultural vacuum of Canaan, with no prestigious monarchies, no national leaders, no glittering cities, the Mesopotamian god race achieved its greatest domination. Every day, tables heavily laden with food were placed in the temples to feed the hungry Canaanite gods and goddesses, and nearly every week, festivals would be held in their honor. But there was no spiritual exaltation in these festivals, only drunken orgies of gluttony and debauchery with the priests and the temple harlots, which supposedly tickled the prurient fancies of the gods. But the food offerings and the debauchery were not enough to appease the Canaanite gods. Only the immolation of children would satisfy the bottomless hunger of the gods, and the people readily complied, throwing their own children into the roaring flames on the altars of their gods.

This then was the land toward which God had directed Abraham. This was the land that God promised to Abraham and his offspring as a consecrated birthright for all time. This was the land upon which Abraham's descendants would erect sanctuaries in which the Divine Presence would reside. This land that would eventually be known to all peoples as the Holy Land was now polluted by the most degenerate and corrupted people in the world. This was the place where Abraham would spend the rest of his life proclaiming the Name of God.

At this point, when God promised to build His chosen nation from among Abraham's offspring and give them the land, Abraham became the patriarch of the Jewish nation. And from this point on, when Abraham was already fairly advanced in years, the Biblical account of his life becomes minutely detailed. The primary purpose of all this detail is, of course, to provide moral and religious instruction rather than historical information; *maasei avos siman levanim*, the deeds of the patriarchs are signposts for their descendants.[5] But the sweep of history nevertheless emerges from between the lines.

When Abraham first arrived in Canaan with his large retinue of followers and his great wealth, he settled near Bethel and assumed his own sovereign status as a minor king in the fragmented political galaxy of Canaan. After a brief visit to Egypt during a period of drought,[6] Abraham returned to Canaan and settled near the Hittite city of Hebron, where he proceeded to publicize his radical views on divinity. While in Hebron, he was instrumental in repelling Amorite armies from Elam and Babylon who had invaded Canaan in retaliation for a lapse in tributary payments,[7] and as a result, his stature and prestige among the local populace were immeasurably enhanced.

Some time after this incident, Abraham carried his message to Gerar, the land of the Philistines, a powerful people whose major cities were Gaza, Ashkelon, Ashdod, Gath and Ekron on the south coastal plain. Abraham signed a peace treaty with the king of Philistia, which further added to his prestige among the peoples of the land. Then he settled in Beersheba in Philistine territory, an important crossroads on the Near Eastern caravan routes, and gained great fame for his hospitality and generosity. All wayfarers who passed through Abraham's open doors would leave with their stomachs filled and their minds set aflame with the idea of an all-powerful, spiritual God who demanded that men lead their lives in a moral fashion.

In Beersheba, Abraham and his wife Sarah had a son late in life, and they named him Isaac. Earlier, Abraham's Egyptian concubine Hagar had borne him a son named Ishmael.[8] Abraham, however, concentrated his efforts on his son Isaac. In a prophetic vision, God had promised him that his descendants would form a great nation with the entire Land of Canaan as their birthright but that this birthright belonged only to the descendants of his son Isaac. The seal of the covenant was the commandment of circumcision, the mark of which would forever be the symbol of God's selection of the descendants of Abraham.

Thus, a very important distinction was established in Abraham's outlook, a distinction between ideology and nation. Abraham would continue to disseminate his views among the Canaanite and the Philistines. By the force of his charismatic personality and the grandeur of his reputation, he would continue to gather about him numerous followers who accepted his views and acknowledged the Creator of the Universe. But at the same time, he would initiate the long and laborious process of building a nation from his own offspring, a nation whose very identity would be predicated on its covenant with God, its guardianship of His Word and its championship of His Ideals. To the world at large, Abraham presented his views as a philosophy and an ideology, but to his own selected offspring, those views would form the practical foundations of a covenanted nationhood, the vessel which would carry his message to all future generations.

In this sense, Abraham was not a revolutionary bent on toppling society and reshaping it according to his own vision. He did not attempt to establish a far-flung empire which would be ruled by his convictions. Rather, he was a patient builder who dedicated his life to creating the indestructible nucleus of a nation that would endure with undiminished vitality long after the empires of his time, with all their ideologies and beliefs, crumbled into dust.

With this in mind, when it came time for Isaac to marry, Abraham would not consider taking a wife for him from among the degenerate Canaanites. Instead, he sought a suitable match among his own noble family in Harran, eventually choosing his virtuous niece Rebecca. Ishmael, on the other hand, was allowed to take an Egyptian bride.

When Abraham died, Isaac became his spiritual successor, dedicating his life to the service of the Creator in the manner he had learned from his illustrious father. Like his father before him, Isaac also had two sons, Jacob and Esau, only one of whom was worthy of becoming his father's successor. The choice fell on the refined and intellectual Jacob, rather than on his older brother Esau who was a wily hunter and a ferocious warrior. Once again, it was Jacob who sought a bride from among Abraham's noble family in Harran, marrying his cousins Leah and Rachel, while Esau married a Hittite princess, a Hivite princess and the daughter of his uncle Ishmael.

Esau deeply resented Jacob's selection as the next patriarch and heir to the land, but the brothers did reach a wary accommodation and parted ways. Esau went to live in the land of Sair, which thereafter came to be known as Edom, and his numerous sons and grandsons formed the nucleus of a new pagan nation. Nevertheless, the malignant resentment among the descendants of Esau continued to fester, particularly among the Amalekites. It would erupt violently in future generations.

Jacob, who assumed the name Israel in his later years, was the third and final common patriarch of the Jewish people. With him, the winnowing process came to an end. All of Jacob's twelve sons were righteous men and worthy successors to their forbears, and they would all become the patriarchs of their own tribes, which would come to bear their names: Reuven, Simon, Levi, Judah, Issachar, Zevulun, Dan, Naphtali, Gad, Asher, Joseph and Benjamin.

The nucleus of the nation was complete. It was a small group but a cohesive one with a proud and exalted tradition who became known as the people of Israel; ultimately, they would become known as the Jews, taking their name from the predominant tribe of Judah. The tiny seed of Israel had been planted and nurtured with infinite care, and from it would emerge a stalwart tree that, despite all the battering and buffeting of hostile winds, would bend but never break.

Isaac and Jacob, unlike Abraham, did not inaugurate revolutionary historic events, but their lives were nonetheless richly textured and minutely examined in the Biblical record. As the second and third Jewish patriarchs, they completed the development of the fundamental Jewish concepts of selfless benevolence, moral fortitude and truth. Thus, although they may have been less significant than Abraham in a narrow historical context, they were certainly comparable in the broader religious context.

During Jacob's old age, another of the periodic droughts brought famine to Canaan. Some time earlier, in one of the most enigmatic Biblical episodes, the young Joseph had been sold into slavery and carried off to Egypt. But Joseph was a thoroughly righteous man and God guided him safely through the perils of captivity. Blessed with extraordinary wisdom and talents, he eventually rose to the high position of viceroy and was entrusted with the management of the economy. Under Joseph's supervision, the royal granaries were filled to overflowing, even as the famine tightened its stranglehold on Canaan. As the famine deepened, the starving Egyptians sold their lands to the crown and even indentured themselves in exchange for grain from the royal reserves. Within a few short years, the pharaoh became the proprietor of all Egyptian landed property, a situation that would endure for close to two thousand years. Joseph's adroit management had brought a tremendous increase of wealth and power to the Egyptian monarchy, and the pharaoh was grateful.

When Jacob's sons came to Egypt to buy food, they discovered that their long-lost brother had become the unofficial ruler of the land, and after an emotional reunion, the entire family went down to Egypt. They were received with great honor by the pharaoh and were granted landhold rights in the land of Goshen in the district of Ramses, where they intended to stay until conditions in Canaan improved. There, Jacob met Joseph's sons, Ephraim and Menashe, for the first time, and he bestowed upon them the status of individual tribes.

Seventeen years later, Jacob died in Goshen. His body was embalmed and taken under an Egyptian royal escort to Canaan, where he was laid to rest alongside his fathers in the city of Hebron. Jacob's death brought to a close the chapter of the patriarchs. A new chapter was about to begin in the land of Egypt.

In the beginning, the stay of the Jews in Egypt was quite a pleasant one. They lived a life of peace and security, and they prospered in the fertile land of Goshen. Unwilling to intermarry or mingle socially with the idolatrous Egyptians, who were steeped in superstition and magic, they kept to themselves, serving the Creator by living moral and ethical lives. After the death of Joseph and the other tribal patriarchs, they continued to thrive and grow in number, eventually becoming a distinct and conspicuous nationality in the otherwise ethnically homogenous Egyptian realm.

Because of its own history, however, Egypt was very xenophobic. Centuries before, at about the time of Abraham's birth, Egypt had been the dominant power of the region, with an ancient dynastic monarchy, a strong central government, a well-organized military and a flourishing economy. Wealthy and stable, Egypt made great advances in agriculture, industry and the military arts, and as a result, its sphere of influence extended far beyond its borders. But then a Syrian people known as the Hyksos conquered the land, overthrew the indigenous pharaohs and ushered in a period of confusion, civil strife and cultural decline. The Hyksos' hold on the Egyptian throne did not last long, and they were driven out about a century before Jacob and his sons arrived. The hereditary Egyptian pharaohs returned to the throne, but the shock of the invasion and occupation of Egypt left its mark on the Egyptian psyche.

At the time of the death of Joseph, the growing presence of the Jews in Goshen constituted the only significant foreign element in Egypt, and peaceful and benign though it was, the wary Egyptians viewed it with suspicion and great foreboding.

Nevertheless, the tribes continued to enjoy the royal protection of the pharaoh, who was deeply grateful to Joseph for his service to the kingdom. But when the next pharaoh came to power, the situation of the tribes took a drastic turn for the worse.

Unencumbered by any feelings of gratitude towards Joseph, the new pharaoh viewed the presence of the Jews with extreme paranoia. What if there were a new invasion of Egypt? Would this burgeoning foreign element in Goshen align itself with the enemy invader? Something had to be done, and the new pharaoh decided on a cunning policy of gradual subjugation.

The first step in the implementation of the policy of oppression was to demand the voluntary participation of the Jewish population in the construction of huge fortifications for the cities of Pithom and Ramses, to which the Jews readily acceded out of gratitude to their Egyptian hosts. But to the dismay of the Egyptians, this gargantuan task did not break the spirit or sap the vitality of the Jews, who continued to enjoy a high birth rate and robust growth.

The Egyptians responded with the complete enslavement of the Jewish people, forcing them to perform all sorts of backbreaking labor under heavy guard in royal construction and agricultural projects, whose primary purpose was to crush the Jews. The exploitation and bondage of the captive Jews deepened and stretched into years and decades, but still, they grew in number and clung tenaciously to the ideas and ideals so painstakingly instilled in them by their forebears. They continued to spurn the gods of the Egyptians, and they fortified themselves against the pernicious influences of the superstitious Egyptian culture by speaking their own Hebrew language, taking only Hebrew names and wearing traditional Jewish garb.

The Egyptian strategy of impoverishment, enslavement and dehumanization now turned to infanticide. Having been told by his astrologers that the birth of a Jewish redeemer was imminent, the pharaoh issued a royal decree that all male Jewish infants were to be killed immediately after birth. With the complicity of the Jewish midwives, however, many Jewish children were snatched from the clutches of the Egyptian executioners and the policy lapsed, but a wave of terror and panic gripped the enslaved people.

The Egyptian policy finally began to achieve its desired effect. After more than a century of grinding persecution, the high-minded idealism and independent spirit of the Jewish people began to wither. Foremost in their minds was to avoid the whips of the overseers, to steal a moment of rest and respite from their never-ending labors, to find a place of refuge for their newborn babes. The crashing tide of affliction eroded their resolve and their pride, and they bowed to the Egyptian masters and gods, falling into a spiritual as well as physical bondage. But at the nadir of the Jewish bondage in Egypt, the wheels of redemption began to turn.

Moses, the greatest prophet and leader of Jewish history, was born to the tribe of Levi during the dark days of Egyptian infanticide. His mother placed him in a basket of reeds and set it adrift in the Nile River in the desperate hope that her precious child would somehow escape the diabolic decree. He was discovered among the bulrushes by the kindhearted daughter of the pharaoh, who was enthralled by the aura of sanctity that enveloped the luminous child. She took the child and brought him up in the relative safety of the palace as a respected member of the royal court. As this divinely ordained savior of the Jewish people grew up, however, he was unable to bear the sight of the affliction of his Jewish brothers. Ultimately, he was forced to flee after striking down an Egyptian overseer who had been thrashing a Jewish laborer.

After wandering from country to country for many years, Moses was told by God in a prophetic vision to return to Egypt and lead the Jewish people to freedom. In his great humility, Moses protested that he was but an inarticulate man unsuited for such an important divine mission, but God reassured him that he would have the full cooperation and assistance of his articulate older brother Aaron. Moses bowed to the Will of God and set out on his mission.

Moses went on to become the greatest man in history. He attained the highest levels of prophecy to the point where he communicated with God "face to face, as one man converses with another,"[9] so to speak. He learned the entire Torah directly from God, and he became the primary teacher of the Torah to the Jewish people and of the moral concepts of the

Torah to the entire world. Accompanied only by his brother Aaron, he confronted the mighty pharaoh in his palace and demanded and eventually obtained the release of his people from a bondage that had lasted for centuries. Yet in spite of his phenomenal greatness and accomplishments, Moses remained "exceedingly humble, more so than any other person on the face of the earth."[10]

The idea of a man being both the greatest and the most humble in the world would seem, at first glance, to be an amazing paradox. Upon reflection, however, there is no anomaly whatsoever.

True humility does not derive from an undervaluation of one's own worth. Rather, it derives from an awareness of the chasm between what one is and what one can be; one contemplates this vast gulf and is humbled by the magnitude of one's own limitations. A person with minimal knowledge and wisdom cannot be truly humble, because he cannot fathom how truly infinitesimal he is in the greater scheme of things. For the same reason, we find that a person becomes more humble as he grows older; the broadening of his scope makes him more acutely aware of his own limitations.

In this light, the superlative humility of Moses is actually an eloquent testament to his superlative greatness. The intellectual and spiritual horizons of his world were far broader than those enjoyed by anyone else, and consequently, he was also more humble than any other person on the face of the earth. This was the man who would lead the Jewish people to freedom and forge them into a nation.

The exodus of the Jewish people from Egypt in the year 1313 b.c.e. under the leadership of Moses, was accompanied by numerous miraculous manifestations, as recorded in vivid detail in the Bible, events which are commemorated annually by the festival of Passover. But the most supernatural event occurred at Mount Sinai when God Himself came down onto the mountain to give the Torah to His chosen people, the descendants of His beloved Abraham, Isaac and Jacob.

Before God had created the world, there had been absolute void, the complete absence of matter, space or even time. Everything was the Infinite Spirit of God, endless, timeless and unbounded. At the time of creation, God had effected a *tzimtzum*, a veiling of His all-pervading Presence so to speak, a partial withdrawal of the Divine Energy which would allow the existence of the material world. But at Mount Sinai, for one brief moment in history, the veil was drawn aside, and the Shechinah, the Divine Presence of God, manifested itself on the mountaintop in full view of the assembled Jewish people.

The mountain and the surrounding land trembled almost to the point of disintegration, not as a result of some specifically directed miracle but by the very nature of what was happening. The entry into the material world of the Divine Presence, of the unrestricted Divine Energy, harkened back to the time before creation, destabilizing the very existence of matter and pushing it to the brink of a return to a state of total material void and infinite spirituality.

Then the Voice of God began to speak the Ten Commandments to the people. But this brought about an even greater escalation of Divine Energy infused directly into the material world, and the people began to faint away to the point of expiration, unable to absorb such pure spirituality without their souls being torn away from their mundane material bodies. The remainder of the Ten Commandments were then transmitted prophetically to Moses, to be repeated to the people in a form they could tolerate physically.

This was the marriage ceremony between God and the Jewish people, the forging of an eternal, indissoluble bond consummated by God Himself appearing to the Jewish people and bestowing upon them the celestial Torah as the nuptial gift that sealed the relationship forever.[11] Both sides pledged their perpetually binding marriage vows. The Jews swore to remain faithful to God and obey His commandments as transmitted to them through Moses, and God swore to bring them into His sanctified land and grant them incalculable blessings if they remained faithful but never to spurn them to the point of extinction even if they slipped into unfaithfulness.

And in the ensuing three thousand years, both sides have remained true to their vows. The core element of the Jewish people has always adhered to the Torah with profound love and strict observance, and God has always protected His people, despite all the misfortune they have brought upon themselves, so that a vital remnant always remained staunch and indestructible. No matter how many Jewish martyrs gave their lives to sanctify the Name, and no matter how many Jews strayed from their own heritage to become submerged and forgotten in other cultures, this vital remnant survived as the inexhaustible fountainhead of the Jewish people.

The memory of this divine ceremony was etched deeply into the national memory of the Jewish people. To a lesser degree, it was also etched into the memories of the surrounding nations that heard reports of these wondrous events, but they did not really understand what was happening. To their way of thinking, a new member of the god race, a god with phenomenal powers, had appeared on the scene as patron of the Jewish people, and they and their own patron gods would clearly have to treat the Jews with deference and respect.

Over the centuries and millennia, however, the full force of the revelation has faded from the memory of mankind, so that in recent times rationalistic historians have begun to contend that it could never have occurred, relegating the story of the exodus to the realm of myth and legend. These historians, who never witnessed such manifestations in their own time, deny the possibility of supernatural or miraculous occurrences.

But a believer in God does not find such things incredible at all. After all, is the God who created the entire world out of the void incapable of performing miracles if He so chooses? And does it not stand to reason that, at one time or another in history, God would choose to reveal His awesome power to the world to such a degree that it would always be remembered? The peoples of the ancient world, and all subsequent generations for thousands of years, believed that this era of divine revelation occurred during the exodus and its aftermath, as reported in the Biblical account. What more appropriate occasion could there have been for such a display than the forging of the eternal bond between God and His chosen people?

At last, the long process of preparation and sublimation initiated by the patriarchs centuries before was complete; the seed planted by the patriarchs had finally sprouted into a full-blown nationhood unlike any other before or after. After over two centuries of the most abject physical and spiritual bondage, the Jews had been elevated from the lowest point of their history directly to their zenith in the very Presence of God. The erstwhile slaves—every man, woman and child—heard the Revealed Word directly from God, while their Egyptian oppressors were humbled and ruined, never again to play a major role in history.

Suffused with the joy and euphoria of their stunning transformation, the emancipated slaves stood before Mount Sinai without any of the conventional trappings of nationhood, with no homeland, no cities, no political institutions, so that the nation forged on that momentous occasion rested solidly on spiritual foundations alone. The cement of the Jewish nation was its special relationship with God, and all other conventional political forms it would eventually assume were only important inasmuch as they served that special relationship. The Jewish nation had been promised a sanctified homeland by God, but it did not need a physical homeland to perpetuate its national identity. Born in exile, it could survive in exile. The Torah was its true homeland.

The Torah the Jewish people received at Mount Sinai was divided into two parts—the Written Torah and the Oral Torah. The Written Torah was comprised of the Pentateuch, the Five Books of Moses, which contained all the laws and commandments; it was eventually expanded to include the prophetic and historical books of the Prophets and the Writings. The practical applications of the laws, however, are not always clear from the verses of the Torah, which are wonders of extreme brevity and sharp impact, unencumbered by voluminous specifics. For instance, the Torah commands the wearing of *tefillin*, but what are *tefillin* and how are they made? Similarly, literally thousands of instructions essential to the proper fulfillment of the commandments do not appear in the written text. Instead, this voluminous body of Torah law was passed down by oral tradition from generation to generation in a parallel adjunct known as the Oral Torah.

Immediately after receiving the Torah at Mount Sinai, the Jewish people began the process of discovering the wonders of this holy and marvelous gift. Employing a chain of instruction based on a Council of Elders, hundreds of thousands of people in their Sinai Desert encampments diligently studied the commandments and moral instructions which guided every aspect of Jewish life, both in the relationship with God and in the relationships with fellow men. The Council of Elders, known as the Sanhedrin, also served as the supreme court in the adjudication of all these matters; it was an institution that would last without interruption for close to two thousand years.

In its totality, the Torah presented an incredibly progressive and sophisticated system, an intensely spiritual religion which addressed and satisfied all social, material, emotional and intellectual needs. It presented a way of life that would be immeasurably fulfilling if followed faithfully, a way of life that could be lived at optimum levels in any situation and environment.

But the Torah is much more than a record of laws, ethics and chronicles. It is the living Word of God, a sublime spiritual life force which God bestowed upon the Jewish people, a life force that would forever course through the veins of the Jewish people and elevate and sustain them for all time. Indeed, the Talmud derides those who rise in the presence of a Torah scroll but not in the presence of a Torah scholar.[12] The Torah scroll, for all its sanctity, is but a reflection of the Torah, while the Torah itself is a divine spirit that lives in the minds and hearts of those who study it. The study of the Torah is not simply a practical exercise which enables a Jew to discover what to do and what not to do, akin to reading a law book. The study of the Torah is the process by which a Jew imbues himself with the divine spirit, and although proper study is of the kind that leads to practical application, the greatest benefit is derived from the act of studying itself, the conduit through which the Jew connects to the supreme life force of the Torah and its Source.

With the Giving of the Torah, Judaism reached its completed form, bringing a sense of purpose and order to the chaotic ancient world. It presented a new concept of divinity and a historical destiny for the entire human race. To the Jewish people in particular, it entrusted the living body of the Torah. If the Jewish people would heed the Torah faithfully, if they would infuse their lives with this celestial life force, if they would become a truly spiritual "light unto the nations," the purpose of creation would be accomplished. At that point, the messianic era would be ushered in, and the Light of God would penetrate to every corner of the world. Only then would strife and hatred be replaced by a boundless, sanctified peace. But until then mankind would continue to grapple with the unresolved struggle between spiritual aspirations and mundane pursuits.

And thus, the Jewish people prepared to enter the Land of Israel over three thousand years ago, a nation built around a sacred body of knowledge and a sophisticated understanding of the world so revolutionary, yet so utterly compelling in its obvious truths, that it ultimately toppled the civilization into which it was born.

3

The Conquest of Canaan

> And I will give to you and to your descen-
> dants the land in which you dwell, the
> entire Land of Canaan, as an eternal
> heritage, and I will be their Lord.
>
> (Genesis 17:8)

The migration of the Jewish people through the wilderness of the Sinai Desert lasted for forty years, during which most of the generation that had emerged from Egypt passed away. Nonetheless, the new generation had grown up in the households of parents who lived through the Exodus and the congregation at Mount Sinai, making the children virtual eye-witnesses to those momentous events. Furthermore, they themselves had heard the teachings and exhortations of Moses. They themselves had studied the Torah in the desert encampments. And as they stood poised to enter Canaan, their hearts were afire with the zeal of anticipated fulfillment. The dream of the Jewish people was about to come true.

The promised land meant much more to the Jewish people than a place to pitch their tents and build their houses, a place to call their own. According to the Torah, the conquest would sanctify the very soil and the air above it. Many of the Torah's commandments consecrated the land and regulated its use; the tithing of grain, for instance, applied only to grain grown on the hallowed soil of Israel. Thus, the conquest of the land would provide the sacred setting where the entire Torah could be fulfilled and the relationship between the Jewish nation and God could be conducted on the highest levels.

But the conquest of Canaan would be no easy matter. Just as the small clan of Jacob's children had grown numerous over the centuries, so had their kindred clans become numerous and powerful. Firmly entrenched on the borders of Canaan, they now blocked the progress of the Jewish people. The Edomites and the Amalekites, descendants of Jacob's brother Esau, occupied the Negev to the south of Canaan. The Ammonites and Moabites, descendants of Abraham's nephew Lot, occupied the lands to the southeast of the Jordan River. The Philistine kingdom sat astride the coastal plain to the southwest of Canaan. The Amorite kingdoms of Cheshbon and Bashan occupied the lands to the east of the Jordan River. Behind this ring of hostile

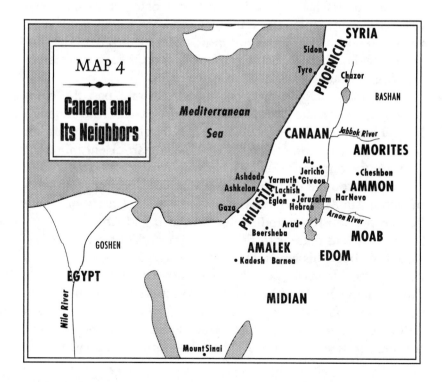

nations, in the land of Canaan itself, the Canaanite people prepared to welcome the new arrivals on the battlefield.

The Jews did not even attempt to pass through Philistia, although that was the most direct route to Canaan. Instead, they veered east and encamped at Kadesh in the Zin Desert on the border of Edom. From there, Moses sent emissaries to the king of Edom requesting permission to pass through Edomite lands and promising to pay for any water the people might use; the Torah had expressly forbidden the conquest of territory from the Edomites, Ammonites or Moabites,[1] and the Jews had no acquisitive designs on these lands. Nevertheless, the Edomite king denied them permission, underscoring his refusal with a show of military might.

Disappointed, the people continued eastward, but their journey was interrupted by an unprovoked attack by the Amalekite king of Arad in the Negev.[2] The Jews had not tried to pass through the Amalekite lands or threatened them in any way, yet the old resentment of Esau towards his brother Jacob still smoldered in the Amalekite soul. The Amalekites had sent an army to attack the Jews in the desert before they had even reached Mount Sinai. The attackers had been repelled during a vicious battle at Refidim, and now, forty years later, they attacked again. The new battle resulted in a decisive Jewish victory and the devastation of the Amalekite cities.

The Jewish people then continued eastward past the cities of Moab, under the jittery surveillance of Balak, the Moabite king. Then they turned north into the deserts of Trans-Jordan on the eastern perimeter of Moab, moving from encampment to encampment until they reached the Arnon River. This river marked the boundary between the Moabite lands and the lands of Sichon, an Amorite king whose capital was in Cheshbon, a city he had previously wrested from neighboring Moab.

As they had done with Edom, the Jews asked for permission to pass through his lands, but Sichon refused their request and chose instead to go to war. The Jewish armies destroyed Sichon's forces in the battle at Yahatz and conquered his entire kingdom, taking possession of Cheshbon and all its satellite towns as well as the Amorite district of Yazeir. From there, they crossed the Yabbok River into the Amorite kingdom of Bashan, where they annihilated the forces of King Og at the battle in Edrei and took possession of the lands.

With the entire Trans-Jordan north of Ammon and Moab now in Jewish hands, the main encampment returned to the Plains of Moab across the Jordan River from Jericho, the eastern gateway to Canaan. The tribes of Reuven and Gad and half the tribe of Menashe chose to settle in the conquered Amorite lands of Trans-Jordan, promising to send troops to assist the rest of the tribes in the conquest of the lands to the west of the Jordan River.

In the spring of 1273 b.c.e., with the Jewish people on the Plains of Moab on the verge of penetrating into Canaan, Moses passed away. Before his death, he had gone up to the summit of Mount Nevo and seen the land which God had promised to his forefathers but on whose hallowed ground he would never tread. As a leader, prophet and teacher of the Torah, he would remain forever unequalled, and all the Jews mourned his loss for thirty days.

The mantle of leadership now passed to his ordained disciple Joshua, a prophet of the tribe of Ephraim. Moses had taken persecuted slaves and forged them into a mighty nation, he had brought them to Mount Sinai to receive the Torah, and he had guided them through forty difficult years in the desert before bringing them to the doorstep of the promised land. It fell to Joshua to complete the task.

Three days after the period of mourning, the Jewish people crossed the Jordan River. They encamped in Gilgal alongside the river on the plains of the great Amorite city of Jericho, and the people celebrated Passover for the first time on their ancestral soil, although it was as yet unconquered.

Immediately after Passover, preparations for war began. The first objective was the capture of Jericho, which dominated the approach routes to the heartland of Canaan. In the face of the impending Jewish invasion, the Amorite garrison of Jericho had been reinforced by battalions from the other Canaanite principalities,[3] and they all now waited behind Jericho's massive fortifications for the anticipated Jewish attack.

Joshua's mission, however, was not only to conquer the land but to purify and sanctify it, to obliterate the loathsome Canaanite culture that had polluted the land. Battlefield victories would not be enough. The land had to be thoroughly cleansed before a society dedicated to God and His Torah could be established on its soil.

From an earlier reconnaissance mission into Jericho, Joshua had learned that the invincible advance of the Jews had struck terror into the hearts of the peoples of Canaan. He now issued a proclamation to the entire land of Canaan, offering its inhabitants three choices. They could leave the land of their own free will, they could surrender and submit to the total dismantling of their culture, or they could go to war.[4] They chose war.

The battle at Jericho launched the War of Conquest, but it was not much of a battle. The Jewish victory was quick and overwhelming. Jericho was completely destroyed, its walls leveled to the ground, not by force of arms but by God Himself, the final climax to an era of unforgettable revelation which had begun with the Exodus and the Giving of the Torah at Mount Sinai.

In the aftermath of the destruction of Jericho, the Girgashites conceded defeat and departed for Africa; there is no further mention of them in the Books of the Prophets.[5] The other nations, however, chose to remain and fight to the finish, hopeless as it seemed.

The fall of Jericho was followed almost immediately by the battle at Ai to the southwest of Jericho. The Jews were again victorious, but this time, the battle took on more conventional forms, with victory coming as a result of excellent strategy and military prowess. The kings of Canaan took this as an encouraging sign; if the Jews were beginning to fight ordinary battles, then perhaps they could be vanquished.[6]

The kings of Canaan were fully aware of the remarkable Jewish victories, which they attributed to the assistance of a powerful member of the god race who had become the patron god of the Jews. But this new god, it seemed, had exhausted his powers with the conquest of Jericho. Henceforth, the war would be fought on equal terms, and for this the Canaanites were prepared. They had numerous troops and war chariots, and they believed they could muster their own gods to fight on their side. There was hope after all, and they formed a confederation to defend their homeland against the invaders.

The Hivites of the large city of Giveon, however, wanted no part of the coming war. They sent a delegation to Joshua in Gilgal offering their unconditional surrender and complete submission, which Joshua accepted. The defection of Giveon was a serious blow to the confederation.

With the confederation in danger of disintegrating, Adonizedek, the Amorite king of Jerusalem, enlisted the help of the Amorite kings of the mountain cities of Hebron, Yarmuth, Lachish and Eglon and laid siege to Giveon. In desperation, the Giveonites appealed to Joshua in Gilgal. Joshua mustered an army and marched through the night, catching the besieging Amorite armies by surprise and annihilating them in a furious battle.

After lifting the siege of Giveon, Joshua's forces pushed on, and in rapid succession, they destroyed all the Canaanite cities and towns in the central plains and mountains. A major Jewish beachhead had been established in the heart of Canaan, but the conquest had just begun.

The tide of war now shifted to the north of Canaan. King Yavin of Chazor in the central plain, the largest and most powerful city in all of Canaan, organized a confederation of the northern cities. They agreed to coordinate their efforts and bring their numerous infantry and chariot brigades to a common encampment at Mei Merom, which would serve as a staging point for the attack on the Jewish forces.

Once again, Joshua used the element of surprise to great advantage by launching a preemptive strike on the encampment at Mei Merom, routing the combined armies of the northern confederation and pursuing the fleeing remnants as far as the Phoenician city of Sidon in Lebanon. The battle at Mei Merom broke the back of the resistance, and from that point on, the onslaught of the Jewish armies under the leadership of Joshua was irresistible. The Jewish armies marched across the length and breadth of Canaan like a fiery storm, bringing the number of petty kingdoms destroyed to thirty-one.

The war was over. Canaan was devastated; most of its population had perished or were scattered to the winds, as far away as Germany and France.[7] Only Philistia in the south and the

Canaanite strongholds in the far north remained unconquered, but for all practical purposes, the land was in the possession of the Jewish people. The conquered lands of Trans-Jordan had already been apportioned by Moses among the tribes of Reuven, Gad and half of Menashe, and now, Joshua apportioned all the lands west of the Jordan River among the other tribes.[8] The tribes took possession of their individual districts and began the process of rebuilding the cities and towns for their own use. God's promise to His people had been fulfilled. The land of Canaan no longer existed. The new land of Israel stood on its decadent ruins.

But the victory of the Jewish people was not complete. The Canaanite civilization had been crushed but not annihilated, and minuscule traces of the old community remained, nestled like dormant germs throughout the conquered territories. Only

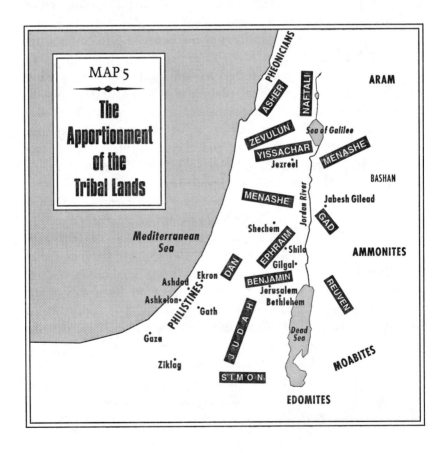

MAP 5

The Apportionment of the Tribal Lands

the tribe of Judah completed the conquest of its own lands, so that none of the Canaanite inhabitants remained.[9] The other tribes were not so successful. Their failure would come back to haunt them in the years and centuries to come.

If anything, however, the failure of the tribes to accomplish the total annihilation of the Canaanite culture reflected on their innate gentleness and nobility of character. As long as war had raged in Canaan, the Jewish armies had sought out and destroyed the Canaanite pockets in the heat of battle, killing the warriors and driving the survivors out of the country. But as the fury of war subsided, the natural Jewish revulsion to slaughter and violence resurfaced, and a return to a peaceful existence seemed more important than dealing with the stubborn Canaanite remnants. The Jewish people had no stomach for further hostilities, and for the most part, they were content to impose heavy taxes on the Canaanite survivors and leave it at that.[10]

It was a serious mistake, and Joshua warned them of its consequences before he died.[11] For although the remaining Canaanites posed no immediate military threat, they were like an abandoned minefield in the aftermath of war, liable to explode at any time. In the long term, they could form the nucleus of a resurgent Canaanite population inside the borders of Israel, creating internal security problems. In the short term, they represented festering little islands of immoral paganism which could only be a hindrance to the establishment of a moral and idealistic Jewish society.

But in the warm glow of their recent victories, the Jewish people were still in a state of euphoria, quite certain that their invincibility, both military and spiritual, would last forever; potential future problems could not be seriously considered in such a rosy state of mind. Foremost in their minds was the exhilarating work of building their new nation.

The prophetically ordained moment had finally come. Five hundred years after Abraham had first set foot in Canaan as a childless exile driven from the land of his birth because of his beliefs and convictions, his multitudinous offspring were returning, consecrated by an everlasting covenant with God, to build the society of his dreams. And the society they established was unlike any other the world had ever seen or would ever see again. For the next four hundred years, the land of Israel was the closest approximation of a utopia that ever appeared on the face of the earth.

A utopian society, in which each individual can aspire to personal fulfillment without threat of injustice and exploitation, has always been the tantalizing ideal of mankind. For thousands of years, philosophers and political theorists have experimented with systems that might achieve the utopian state. And every single one of them has failed, because they were all predicated on a naive faith in mankind's innate goodness. But man is not inherently good. He is inclined to "evil from his earliest youth,"[12] and without proper breeding and guidance, he is by nature a feral and voracious beast, the most dangerous creature alive. Therefore, a society without laws and controls is automatically doomed to chaos, and a society with laws and controls is doomed to abuse by its corruptible lawmakers and controllers. And thus, a utopia created by men is unattainable.

The Torah, however, because of its divine origin and its unlimited legal scope, provided a real opportunity to create a utopian society. Since every aspect of individual and community life is regulated by the Torah to one degree or another, a society governed by the Torah need only appoint judges to apply the laws but not lawmakers to formulate them. The individual can then flourish in a structured society, protected by the law from the avaricious designs of his neighbors and protected from abuse by the law itself by its very nature and divine origin. Thus, utopia on earth was within reach of the Jewish people if only they would collectively resolve to accept the Torah and abide by its jurisdiction.

But once again, the inevitable failings of human nature bring this prospect into question. After all, how can this spirit of communal resolve be sustained over a long period of time? What happens to this inspired resolve when desire and greed rear their ugly heads? What is to prevent man's natural "inclination to evil" from causing a breakdown in the system? The solution to this problem also lies in the Torah itself.

As previously explained, the Torah was given in two parts,

the Written Torah containing all the essentials and the Oral Torah containing all the details and clarifications. Understandably, the voluminous specifics of the Oral Torah could not have been incorporated into the brief and sharply delineated verses of the Written Torah. But the question arises, why could they not have been written down as a separate explanatory body of law distinct from the Written Torah itself, as indeed they were during the Talmudic period? Why did the transmission of these laws have to remain oral as long as possible? There are a number of answers to this question, all of which are valid in their own right.

One important benefit of not having a written record is exclusivity. Judaism is not an evangelical religion, and it does not seek the conversion of the gentiles; in fact, the Talmud requires that prospective gentile converts be dissuaded, if at all possible.[13] According to the teachings of Judaism, gentiles are only required to lead moral and ethical lives according to the guidelines of the Seven Noachide Laws.[14] The six hundred and thirteen commandments of the Torah apply only to the Jewish people who have been singled out as a priestly caste, a role that carries both privilege and obligation.

From the perspective of Judaism, there is therefore no advantage to be gained from exposing the Torah to the critical and often hostile scrutiny of the gentiles who have been excluded. Only harm can come from such a thing. The Talmud considers the translation of the Written Torah into Greek during the post-Alexandrian period to have been a dark episode in Jewish history.[15] Certainly, the exposure of the Oral Torah would have been considered an even greater breach.

Therefore, the absence of a written record safeguarded the proprietary exclusivity of the Torah for a thousand years, and only when historical developments threatened the oral record did the Sages allow the Oral Torah to be written down.

Furthermore, the absence of a written record insured the integrity of the Oral Law, because it could only be learned from a living teacher and not from the pages of a book. The Oral Law is full of nuances and subtleties that are critical to a correct application of the law, and these finer points are often lost on the self-taught student who does not have the advantage of dialogue with an seasoned teacher and hands-on experience. For example, let us assume that two young men of equal talent decided to become surgeons. One of them went to medical school, while the other secured a full set of medical books and the use of a laboratory. Which one would we employ if we needed surgery? No answer is, of course, required. Application of the Oral Law is no less a fine art than surgery, and the absence of a written record guaranteed a tradition of teacher-student relationships.

Finally, the absence of a written record helped reinforce the singular character of Jewish life. God had commanded the Jewish people to study the Torah "day and night,"[16] to plunge into its endless depths and extract its intellectual and spiritual treasures. The ideal condition of the Jew is to be connected constantly to the divine life force of the Torah, either through the direct conduit of study or through the practical performance of its commandments and the conduct of everyday affairs according to its guidelines. The absence of a written record of the Oral Law pushed the Jew in this direction, because every Jew had to spend a good portion of his waking hours studying, memorizing and reviewing the laws that governed all aspects of Jewish life.

This then is the ideal Jewish life. It is an all-consuming attachment to God through His Torah, either through study or performance. It is an attachment that is supposed to be continual from early childhood to the moment of death, without any interruption whatsoever. Ideally, the Jew has no "spare" time in the sense of disposable time. Everything he does is goal-oriented. He eats and sleeps because he needs strength. He works because he must support his family. He rests or plays because he must give himself a respite so that his intellectual and emotional circuits do not overheat.

Unlike the pagan who gives his gods their due and then turns inward to indulge himself, the Jew views his life as a single integrated totality. In spite of all the inevitable sputters and dips, the composite life of a Jew is directed toward the attainment of an elevated state of the spirit, toward perfect attachment to God. The cement that holds this integrated and inspired Jewish life together is the Torah.

As the Jewish people concluded the conquest of Canaan and prepared to build the new nation of Israel, this was the ideal toward which they strove. At that moment, they stood on the threshold of the most extraordinary achievement in the history of mankind. They were about to create a society in which the transcendent aspiration of each individual member was the common selfless goal of achieving perfect unity between God and His people. They were about to create a society in which the benevolent light of Torah would shine upon every aspect of individual and communal life. They were about to create a utopia.

The generation of the Conquest was a generation of pioneers, not only in the territorial sense but in the spiritual sense as well. They plunged into the task of nation-building with the kind of blazing zeal that only pioneers can muster. They were God's soldiers entrusted with a divine mission, and nothing would stand in their way. The physical work was not exceedingly great; the wartime damage to the cities had to be repaired, but the groves, orchards and cultivated fields were largely intact. The main effort was directed toward molding a model society according to the Torah blueprint, in creating new life patterns by which one could aspire to fulfillment.

The new life patterns were, of course, centered around the Torah. The primary occupation of every Jew, outside of earning a livelihood or attending to home and hearth, was the study of the Torah and the practical application of its commandments. Every Jewish child could read the Written Torah and understand most of it; even in the early Biblical period, there was virtually universal literacy among the Jewish people, something totally unheard of among the gentiles in the ancient world or, for that matter, at any time until the very recent past. Furthermore, every Jew had at least some degree of proficiency in the Oral Torah as well, which he acquired from his teachers who had acquired it from their own teachers in the sanctioned chain of instruction reaching back to Mount Sinai.

The common people, for the most part, studied the laws that applied to the agricultural produce of Israel, which could not be eaten before the tithes and charitable portions were separated, the dietary laws and the laws of ritual purity. They also studied the myriad laws that governed all Jewish activity on the Sabbath and the annual cycle of festivals. A solid working knowledge of these vast areas of Torah law was absolutely necessary for every Jewish man and woman in order to function in society, and thus, the long and difficult process of learning, understanding and memorization began from early childhood.

Those people with a greater scholarly capacity would go beyond these basic areas of law and study the full scope of civil and business law, marital and family law and the laws of the holy service. Very often, these people became rabbis and judges, but this was not necessarily so. Jews from all walks of life were required to know as much about all areas of the Torah as they could possibly absorb, even if their acquiring this knowledge would serve no practical purpose for them or for anyone else. The study of Torah *lishmah*, for the sake of the study itself, is the highest form of Torah scholarship, and thus, it was not uncommon for farmers, merchants or laborers to have a thorough knowledge of the Torah.

Most of the people who reached a high level of Torah scholarship eventually became teachers in their own right, either in a public forum or within the narrower confines of their own homes and families. A small number of people became acknowledged experts in a particular area of the Torah, and questions of students and teachers from their towns and districts would be directed to them for resolution. An even smaller number of people became experts in the entire Torah. They were the *gedolei hador*, the greatest of the generation, and some of them actually achieved the gift of prophecy. The judges of the Sanhedrin, the highest Torah court, were drawn from among these men and served as the final authority on all questions of Torah law. Thus, any confusion or omission that might arise as a result of the process of oral transmission could always be rectified by the learned prophets of each generation.[17]

The Jewish people thus became a nation of Torah scholars, which resulted in a far deeper social metamorphosis that mere acceptance of the authority of the Torah would have accomplished. Moreover, they became scholars of the highest order, because their field of study was divine law as prescribed by the Word of God rather than natural law as manifested in the physical world that presented itself to the human eye.

In the natural sciences, all discoveries are not ends in themselves but stepping stones to subsequent discoveries. The discovery of electricity was certainly a tremendous scientific breakthrough in its time, but in our own times, it is taken for granted. Therefore, if we were to duplicate today the study that led to the discovery of electricity it would be considered a waste of time. On the other hand, if the Torah studies of the early settlers of Israel were to be transplanted to our own times they would be considered as vibrant and current as ever.

The scholarship of the Jewish people was, therefore, a living, timeless scholarship that was not restricted to the finite boundaries of the physical world. It was a scholarship that bound the people to their Creator, that refined their characters and elevated their souls.

Among such a nation of Torah scholars, there was no room for violence or intemperance or promiscuity. Indeed, so deeply did the early generations impress this imprint upon the national character that until this very day the Jewish people have remained a gentle and sober nation of scholars. And although even dedicated scholars are only human, succumbing to their desires and instincts from time to time, these failings remain restricted to the personal struggles of the individual. They do not become endemic to the society, and they are not likely to cause a breakdown in the social system.

At the center of this refined society of Torah scholars, the Divine Presence resided, so to speak, in the inner sanctum of the Mishkan, the portable Sanctuary in which the Tablets of the Ten Commandments had been transported from Mount Sinai through the wilderness for forty years. During the apportionment of the land, the Mishkan was installed at Shilo in the land of the tribe of Ephraim, which became the priestly capital of Israel; it would remain there for nearly four centuries before the Holy Temple in Jerusalem would be built by King Solomon.[18] For the Jewish people, the Mishkan was the center of their society, of their nation, of the entire universe. It was the small point of contact between the physical earth and the purely spiritual world of Heaven which they had glimpsed for a fleeting moment during the revelation of the Divine Presence at Mount

Sinai after their exodus from captivity in Egypt.

In this House of God, the Jewish people encountered the Creator through the rituals of the sacrificial service. But this sacrificial service was as different from pagan sacrifices as day is different from night. Pagan temple service was not a spiritual experience; the people would sacrifice animals to feed the appetites of their hungry gods, and having appeased their gods, they would celebrate with drunken orgies and all sorts of self-indulgent revelry. But in the Mishkan, the Jewish people would come to cement and perpetuate their special spiritual relationship with God.

Any relationship needs concrete expression to keep it alive. A friendship will not blossom if it is not bolstered by concrete expression through acts of friendship. Emotions that are only expressed through lip service will eventually wither away. Thus, in order to give substance and permanence to the Jewish spirit, the Jewish people needed to give symbolic expression to their total attachment to the Creator. The sacrificial service provided that opportunity.

Before he brought a sacrifice, the Jew repented from his sins and cleansed his soul of its spiritual defilement. Only then could he offer up the sacrifice in accordance with the meticulously prescribed ritual, as if to say, "I am ready to offer myself up to You with love and reverence, to give myself wholly to You, heart, mind, body and soul. May it be Your Will that this consecrated animal I am sacrificing on the holy altar be accepted in my stead as if I had been the sacrifice." And as the officiating priests sprinkled the blood on the corners of the altar, the soul of the Jew was spiritually elevated, for he had given symbolic expression to his feelings.

The performance of all the commandments are, of course, also expressions of the Jew's relationship with God, but only in the Mishkan could he actually give a gift to God, and that gift was himself. Similarly, the daily communal sacrifices and the supplementary sacrifices on special occasions were also expressions of the desire of the people to offer themselves up collectively to God with love and devotion.

In our own times, these practices are sometimes derided as barbaric and inhumane. But quite the opposite is true. The sacrificial service represented the epitome of civilization, the complete spiritual and material submission of the human being to God through the symbolic act of animal sacrifice.

Even today, with the Jewish people in exile, the concept of the sacrifice still endures through the daily prayers, the uttering of whose words is considered a humble substitute for the sacrifices which can no longer be brought.[19] But this is no more than a pale shadow of the actual sacrifices, the supreme tangible symbol of the eternal bond between God and the Jewish people.

And thus, in this land of Torah scholars among whom the Divine Presence resided, an amazing aberration of history occurred, a phenomenon that lasted for four centuries. For the first four hundred years of its existence, the land of Israel did not have a national government; the only official bodies were the Sanhedrin and its bailiffs who administered civil justice and religious law and the local charities and community service organizations mandated by the Torah. There was no monarchy, no ministries, no political institutions, no standing army, no nationwide system of taxation. God was the King of Israel, and His Torah was the law of the land. The Jewish people had created a potential utopia.

4

Centuries of Troubled Utopia

> *And I will restore to you judges as you*
> *once had and advisors as from the begin-*
> *ning, then you will be called a city of*
> *justice, a faithful bastion.*
>
> *(Isaiah 1:26)*

topia is a state of mind, and history has shown that it is a practically unattainable ideal. As long as people strive towards a goal, as long as they grasp at a dream, they rise far above the ordinary human condition. They become pioneers, and pioneers are an altogether different breed. Pioneers are galvanized by the passionate pursuit of their dreams, and they will let nothing stand in their way. They are prepared to sacrifice personal comfort and safety, they do not hesitate to endure pain and privation, and they can reach inside themselves for strength and courage that ordinary people do not seem to have. But once they reach their goals, once their dreams become reality, they cease to be pioneers. Once again, they become ordinary people with ordinary vices and failings.

In one form or another, this has happened again and again throughout history. Indeed, it is one of the most common underlying causes of the rise and fall of empires. As long as an empire is on the rise, its leaders and people are strugglers and builders driven by a vision and a goal; they are courageous, resourceful pioneers who transcend the weaknesses of ordinary men. But once the empire is built, the pioneering spirit departs. Then the habitual human failings and corruption reappear, and the disintegration begins.

In this century, we have witnessed the misguided attempt to create a communist utopia. From the middle of the nineteenth century, the concept of a classless materialistic society captured the imagination of idealistic youth until the movement became an almost irresistible historical imperative. Men and women were willing to sacrifice, to struggle, to lay down their very lives for the communist dream. But once the revolutionary communist governments were installed in Russia and China, the visionaries virtually vanished. From then on, it was every man for himself. Corruption and disillusionment replaced hope and idealism. And in the end, all attempts to stimulate a perpetual pioneering spirit, such as the Chinese Cultural Revolution of 1965,[1] were dismal failures. Once a goal has been reached, the pioneering spirit can no longer be artificially sustained.

The utopian society of ancient Israel, however, broke this pattern of history. Although it benefitted immeasurably from the pioneering spirit of the settlers, ancient Israel did not go into decline once it was established. Remarkably, it endured for four hundred years as a free society without a political government, a society in which "every man did as he pleased."[2] The pioneering spirit waned and waxed over the centuries, yet it never completely disappeared.

Why was this so? What was so different about ancient Israel that its pioneering spirit was not extinguished for centuries after its establishment? The answer to this question goes to the very heart of Judaism.

The life of the ideal Jew is delineated by numerous concrete goals. He aspires to certain levels of Torah scholarship, of quality in religious performance, of introspection in prayer, of sensitivity and selflessness in personal relationships. Having achieved these goals, his sights immediately rise to the next levels, and he begins to pursue a new set of goals. Ultimately, the ideal Jew strives to know the entire Torah in all its boundless breadth and depth, and by living according to the Torah, he strives to approach a perfect existence of pure spirituality, to emulate God so to speak. These goals are, of course, unattainable, yet the constant striving to reach them produces excellence of the highest order.

The ideal Jew, therefore, is a perpetual pioneer in his personal life. He is always pursuing a dream, always struggling to break through barriers, always climbing higher peaks, always prepared to sacrifice, to suffer, to reach back for his last ounce of strength and endurance. This is the profile of a righteous person in the Jewish concept.[3] The righteous jew is identified by his relentless mental attitude, by his direction more than by his accomplishments. He is always growing, always improving, always a pioneer.

The collective pioneering spirit that built the utopian society of ancient Israel drew its sustenance from this wellspring of individual pioneerism. The purpose of a society in which each individual enjoyed freedom and security was not simply to allow the individual to pursue personal pleasures and indulgences. It was to allow him to pursue the personal goal of forging a perfect bond with the Creator through the conduit of His Torah. Consequently, the collective goal of creating a utopian society was merely a stepping stone to a higher individual goal, and although the collective goal was reachable, the individual goal was not. Thus, there was always an underlying unrealized goal in the utopian society of ancient Israel which kept the pioneering spirit alive.

In the short term, however, the pioneering spirit did flicker and sputter on more than one occasion. The first settlers were immensely inspired by the wonders of the Conquest, and they proceeded to build the new society with zeal and dedication. But as time passed and a new generation grew up, the national zeal diminished, and a feeling of complacency spread through the land.

To be sure, the idealistic fires still blazed within the righteous people who continuously pursue goals of personal excellence. But their struggles became personal battles fought in the privacy of their homes and their hearts, and they failed to energize the many unlearned people who did not have any particularly high-minded goals of their own. And as a result, once the collective goal was reached, these simple people were left with no transcendent goals at all. No longer charged by a pioneering spirit, they now became vulnerable to the pagan influences of the Canaanites who had remained in the land. They became the chink in the armor of the Jewish people.

For the first years of its existence, ancient Israel was secure within its borders in spite of the ring of hostile nations that surrounded it. Although outnumbered by their enemies, the Jewish people were so motivated and inspired that none of their neighbors considered it feasible to attack them. But even more, Israel represented the Kingdom of God on earth, and it stood among its pagan enemies like an impregnable citadel with the Torah at its heart and a host of angels standing guard over it.

As the pioneering spirit waned, however, the simple people found themselves adrift, their lives devoid of the compelling force of idealism. Under normal circumstances, this would not necessarily have been a cause for alarm. It would certainly have been unrealistic to expect every single Jew to be a heroic spiritual warrior. Had the weaker elements remained faithful to the Torah, taking pleasure in the joys of Jewish life, overall Jewish society would not have suffered. But circumstances were not normal. Little pockets of paganism still festered in the land, residue from the uncompleted conquest, and now, the seductive blandishments of pagan life began to penetrate the formerly impregnable Jewish citadel. The failure to complete the conquest had come back to haunt the Jewish people.

Little by little, the social barriers between the Jews and the Canaanites began to crumble. Fraternization with the Canaanites no longer seemed like such a terrible thing. The initially tentative social contacts led to closer associations and friendships. The more daring among the Jewish friends of the Canaanites even began to attend the celebrations in the Canaanite temples, which were invariably characterized by debauchery and promiscuity. Slowly, they were drawn into the vortex of carnal pleasures until they began to intermarry with the Canaanites and worship in the Canaanite temples. Although even these simple Jews knew full well that "there was no substance to the pagan religions, they turned to idolatry in order to join in the public orgies."[4] For the flesh is undeniably weak, and without powerful spiritual defenses, the appetites of the flesh cannot be resisted.

Once the spiritual defenses of the nation were breached, there were no other defenses to control the pagan influences. The judicial system could only deal with individual cases under the meticulous rules of evidence spelled out in the Torah; it was not designed for use as a political instrument to combat a national malaise. And in this aspiring utopian society, there was no government to exercise the political options of prevention and control.

The damage was done. An unholy cancer began to grow in the sanctified body of ancient Israel, eating away at the weak edges of society. All strata of Jewish life suffered. The conspicuous presence of the idolatrous Jews stole the enchantment from the Sabbath and the festivals and poisoned the environment in which Jewish children were being raised. The cancer was sapping the vitality of the Jewish nation and slowly destroying it.

The situation grew progressively worse. Israel was corrupted and decaying, a rudderless ship with no internal solidarity or sense of purpose, and its hostile neighbors did not fail to notice.

The first attack on the new Jewish nation came from the north. In 1245 b.c.e., Israel was invaded by King Cushan of the upstart Syrian principality of Aram. The formerly invincible Jewish nation, which only twenty-eight years before had crushed the Canaanite confederations, now fell helplessly before the Aramean conquerors. Glorious Israel had become the enslaved satellite of a third-rate power. The Jewish people were still free to practice their own religion if they so chose, since the pagans were always generous in making room for new additions to the god race. But under the Aramean military government of occupation, they lost their personal liberties, and they were economically oppressed and impoverished.

The connection between the internal disintegration of Jewish society and its military defeat was not lost on the Jewish people. Before he died, Joshua had cautioned them against such an eventuality. At that time, the people had made a covenant with Joshua, solemnly declaring their unswerving allegiance to God and His Torah. But they did swerve, and it cost them dearly.

Belatedly, they cried out to the God of their fathers in anguish and mortification. But short of an outright miracle, what could be done? The delicate balance of society had been destroyed. The land was a spiritual and physical shambles occupied by foreign troops. How could the process of renewal begin?

The answer came in the form of a man from the tribe of Judah named Asniel ben Kenaz, one of the Elders of the Sanhedrin, a brilliant prophet with an encyclopedic knowledge of the Torah. Asniel ben Kenaz was the acknowledged *gadol hador*, the leading Torah sage of the generation, and immediately after the Aramean invasion, he took upon himself the mission of revitalizing the Jewish people.

For the next eight years, Asniel ben Kenaz rebuked the Jewish people for their transgressions and exhorted them to rededicate themselves to God and His Torah. In cities, towns and villages across the land, he made fiery speeches to increasingly larger assemblies of Jews from all walks of life, alternately reprimanding and cajoling, chastening and inspiring. Slowly but surely, even the simplest people began to rediscover the shining spirit that had electrified the generation of their fathers. Slowly, the shimmering utopian goals of yesteryear emerged from among the clouds of confusion, and once again, all the Jewish people became pioneers with a divine mission and a gallant quest.

During all this time, the Aramean government of occupation did not interfere with Asniel ben Kenaz's spiritual crusade, because his oratory had no political content. But under their very eyes, the fragmented and demoralized Jews were being transformed into a cohesive and inspired people. Under their very eyes, Asniel ben Kenaz was mobilizing a Jewish revolt whose secret weapon would be the Torah.

Eight years after the Aramean invasion, preparations for the Jewish revolt were complete. Idolatry and pagan associations were expunged from among the Jewish people, and the national zeal for Torah had been rekindled. In 1237 b.c.e., under the leadership of Asniel ben Kenaz, the oppressed people of Israel revolted and expelled the invaders, and once again, peace and prosperity returned to the land.

Throughout all these events, Asniel ben Kenaz had never

held any official political position. He had mobilized and led the revolt without any formal authority. His leadership was not sanctioned by the might of the law but by the moral power of his message. The unofficial designation he bore was Shofet, or Judge, which reflected his role as a holy sage who judged the actions of his people and rebuked them for their transgressions. Moses and Joshua had been kings according to Torah law,[5] but Asniel ben Kenaz was the first informal Judge.

Through his personal stature and the force of his personality, Asniel ben Kenaz had brought the Jewish people back from the brink of disaster. He had restored a society which was governed by God and His Torah, a society which enjoyed perfect justice, unrestricted personal liberties and the absence of political institutions. For the moment, utopia had been recaptured.

The new lease on utopia, however, lasted only thirty-two years until the death of Asniel ben Kenaz.[6] With the passing of the great sage, the earlier patterns repeated themselves, triggering a cycle which would regulate the next three centuries of Jewish history. As society degenerated, it would fall victim to invasion by one or more hostile neighbors. This would bring the people back to their senses, and they would turn to the leading sage of the time, who was traditionally called the Judge of Israel. The Judge would then repair the spiritual damage to society, rally the people around the Torah and lead them to victory. Another interlude of utopia would then return for the remainder of that Judge's life, after which the cycle would usually start again.

Ultimately, these centuries came to be known as the Period of the Judges, during which each of the tribes contributed a Judge to the nation at one time or another.[7] The society during the upturns of this cyclical period would always represent the best times of Jewish history, except for a brief segment of the subsequent Period of the Kings. The Judges of Israel themselves became the models for the great sages who would be the unofficial leaders of the Jewish people in exile. In all times, the core element of the Jewish people, steadfastly faithful to the Torah, would follow the leading Torah sages of the generation on all matters, although the Torah did not specifically require them to do so. The history of this period had shown the wisdom of accepting their counsel and leadership.

For the first three hundred years of the Period of the Judges, the intermittent attacks had come from relatively minor powers who had capitalized on the internal decay of Jewish society. Philistia, however, was an altogether different story.

Philistia was a militaristic confederation of the five powerful cities of Gaza, Ashkelon, Ashdod, Gath and Ekron, each with its own king and military establishment. The Philistines had been entrenched on the south coastal plain since before the days of Abraham. In the days of Moses, the Jewish people coming out of the desert had given Philistia a wide berth out of respect for its military prowess. During the Conquest, the Jews were unable to make any inroads into Philistia, which had been part of the portion promised to the tribe of Judah.

Over the centuries, the Philistines sat in their great fortified cities and warily watched the progress of events in Israel. On two occasions, they made tentative military moves against Israel. There were sporadic border clashes during the times of Shamgar ben Anas, and they had sent troops to reinforce the Ammonite invasion during the times of Jephte. For the most part, however, they were content to bide their time as they consolidated their power and planned the subjugation of Israel. And when Israel once again fell into internal disarray after the death of Avdon, the third of the peacetime Judges, the Philistines decided that at last the time was ripe for an all-out attack.

In 950 b.c.e., the Philistines mounted their first major assault on the heartland of Israel, quickly overrunning the country. With typical Philistine military order, the occupation government installed a chain of armed garrisons across the land, clasping the entire country in an iron military grip. The victory was complete, establishing a Philistine territorial hegemony over Israel that would lead to nearly a century of bloodshed, misery and exploitation. It would also spark fundamental changes in Jewish society.

For the first two decades of Philistine occupation, the subjugation of the Jewish people was widespread and pervasive, with no Judge to galvanize and inspire the people. Prospects brightened somewhat in 930 b.c.e. with the emergence as Judge of a dynamic new leader named Samson, a man of exceptional saintliness and legendary physical strength. For the next two decades, Samson rebuked the people and restored their spirit, while at the same time, he harassed the Philistines to the point of intolerance. But he was not successful in cleansing Jewish society of its pagan contamination.

In 910 b.c.e., Samson destroyed the Philistine city of Gaza during a great convocation of all the leaders of Philistia. Samson himself perished in the process, but most of the Philistine ruling class perished along with him. The Philistine stranglehold on Israel was loosened. Nevertheless, there was no popular uprising, and Israel continued to be a Philistine satellite. The military occupation was lifted, but the Philistine administrators remained in place.

After the death of Samson, Eli the Priest assumed the mantle of Judge of Israel,[10] while he concurrently continued to perform the duties of High Priest in Shilo. In 891 b.c.e., a Jewish army was mustered and sent out to intercept one of the periodic Philistine incursions into Israel. The two armies clashed at Even Haezer. The Jews did not fare well in the initial skirmishes, and they withdrew to regroup.

On the advice of the Elders, they brought the Ark of the Covenant, which contained the original tablets of the Ten Commandments, from the Mishkan in Shilo to the battlefield. They hoped that the presence of the Torah in their midst would make the Jewish fighters invincible, as it had in the past. But in the past the Torah had filled their hearts and their minds; it had been the focal point of Jewish society. Now, however, the glorious spirit was gone. The people were downtrodden and demoralized, and many of them were openly worshipping in the Canaanite temples. The shining spiritual citadel of yesteryear was in ruins, and the physical presence of the Torah was no more than a poor substitute not very likely to turn the tide of battle in their favor.

The arrival of the Ark did indeed frighten the Philistine forces, but they did not break and run. Instead, they fought with a furious and desperate resolve, gaining a stunning victory. They also captured the Ark from the fleeing Jews and carried it off to the Philistine city of Ashdod.

The news of the capture of the Ark was too much for the aged Eli to bear, and he collapsed and died.[11] Samuel of the tribe of Ephraim, Eli's personal ward, now assumed the role of Judge. Samuel's fiery character and prophetic powers were already renowned throughout Israel even during Eli's lifetime, and when he rose to the spiritual leadership of the nation, Samuel became the greatest Judge of the entire Period of the Judges—and the last.

In the meantime, the Philistines suffered a series of calamities that were clearly attributed to the fearsome presence of the Ark in their midst. After a nerve-racking seven months, it was returned to Israel.

Seizing on the opportunity of the national trauma caused by the temporary loss of the Ark, Samuel plunged into his mission with a burst of frenetic energy. He travelled from city to city and exhorted the people to destroy the idols which had infiltrated Jewish society and return as one nation to God and the pure Judaism of their ancestors.

The words of the fiery prophet penetrated to the hearts of the oppressed people. Even during the utopian periods in the days of the earlier Judges, the decontamination had always left minuscule traces of idolatry, but now, there was no holding back. The seemingly endless Philistine occupation was more than even the lowest elements among the Jews were willing to bear, and every last vestige of idolatry was finally eradicated from the land.[12]

The cycle was beginning to come around again, but the wheels of destiny were creaking slowly. Jewish society had been deeply corrupted by the inroads of paganism before and during the Philistine occupation, and it would take many years of hard work to purify and elevate the people, to rekindle the universal pioneering spirit that had characterized the last period of utopia nearly a century before. The will to recapture the precious past was there, but profound spiritual transformations are not effected by a snap of the fingers.

At the behest of the prophet, a vast assembly of the entire nation was convened at Mitzpah[13] for the purpose of prayer, public fasting and a revival of the national spirit. The Philistines, with their keen appreciation for Jewish history, interpreted this convocation as a provocative act in preparation for war, and they responded by sending an army into Jewish territory. The Jews sent an army from Mitzpah to engage the advancing Philistine forces.

The two armies met again on the battlefield at Even Haezer. This time, the Jews dealt the Philistines a devastating blow, and there were no further Philistine military incursions for the remainder of Samuel's life. Another clamp of the occupation had been loosened, but the Philistine civilian administrators still remained in place. The Jews were not yet ready for a total uprising and all-out war with Philistia.

For the next ten years, Samuel continued his activist leadership, crisscrossing the country to judge and instruct the people and to inspire them with his fiery addresses. He also enlisted his two learned sons, Joel and Aviah, to assist him in his duties as Judge, but they were more inclined to remain with their criers and scribes in their judicial headquarters in Beersheba and wait for the people to come to them.[14]

As Samuel grew old, apprehension about the future spread across the land. In spite of the cessation of hostilities, Israel still remained subservient to its powerful Philistine neighbor. To the east, the Ammonites under King Nachash were once again making belligerent threats against the Jewish settlements in Trans-Jordan.[15] The crises that loomed on the horizon demanded superb leadership, and the people questioned the leadership qualities of Samuel's sons. No other potential Judge remotely approaching Samuel's stature seemed to be waiting in the wings. The Elders, therefore, approached Samuel and requested that he institute a hereditary monarchy in Israel, patterned after the prevailing system of government among the other nations of the region.

The request of the Elders disturbed Samuel profoundly, although the idea of a Jewish monarchy was certainly not new. In his prophetic definition of the roles of the tribes, Jacob had designated the tribe of Judah as the fountainhead of kings,[16] and indeed, the Torah had expressly commanded that a king be appointed after the conquest and settlement of the land.[17] But the Biblical concept of a king was totally different from the king the Elders were requesting.

At first glance, one might deem the need for a strong leader most critical during the difficult periods of conquest and settlement. Nevertheless, in the prescribed order of events, the appointment of the king comes only after the conquest and settlement have been accomplished. Clearly, the intended purpose of the king was not military, political or administrative. Clearly, the appointment of a king was intended for a higher, religious purpose.

The high points of the Period of the Judges had proven conclusively that there was no need for political institutions in an ideal society governed by the Torah; the Word of God, as contained in the Torah, provided all the laws and controls society needed. The problem was in perpetuating a universal pioneering spirit that would keep all Jews focused on the ultimate goal of bonding with the Creator. The Judges had been able to accomplish this, to a limited extent, by virtue of their personal stature and moral leadership. The establishment of the monarchy, as mandated by the Torah, would take the traditional but unofficial Judgeship and make it permanent and hereditary.

The anointed Jewish king, therefore, was to be an inspiring religious leader who would lead the people across the last frontiers of the spirit. Just as it was the duty of the High Priest to direct the *avodah*, the temple service, it would be the duty of the king to direct the personal *avodah* of all Jews. And by doing so, the anointed Jewish king would bring about the fulfillment of destiny and usher in the messianic age.

For this reason, the appointment of a king was to be postponed until after the conquest and settlement had been accomplished. As long as society had political and temporal needs, the chosen king could easily slip into the political role of the contemporaneous king models, diverting the king from his religious duties and making Israel vulnerable to the corruption that plagues all political governments. Once the utopian society had been created, however, once the Jewish people had put their house in order and focused on the higher religious goals of the Torah, the time would be ripe for the appointment of a king who would lead them to their rendezvous with their historical destiny.

During the Period of the Judges, serious consideration had never been given to a monarchy. The Judges had never felt that the nation was ready for a Jewish king. With Canaanites still living in Israel, the conquest of the land could not really be considered complete. And despite the cyclical reappearance of a utopian Torah society, the constant backsliding underscored its fundamental instability. The Jewish people had never succeeded in truly permeating all strata of society with the perpetual pioneering spirit of the righteous Jews. According to the dynamics of the cycle, therefore, political and military problems were still inevitable, and consequently, Israel was not yet ready for a king. The king was to be used as the *makeh bepatish*, the final strike of accomplishment. He was too delicate and corruptible an instrument to be used prematurely.

But the Philistine War had brought the Jewish people to the brink of despair. The great Samuel himself, for all his victories and successes, had been unable to rid Israel of the Philistines. It would undoubtedly take a succession of Judges of Samuel's stature to accomplish the total revitalization of Jewish society, and not even one such man was waiting in the wings. The people lost confidence in the traditional system of the Judges, which no longer seemed to hold the key to the salvation of Israel. With the death of Samuel, society would inevitably deteriorate, and Israel would be hopelessly crushed under the yoke of Philistine oppression.

With all this in mind, the Elders approached Samuel and asked him to appoint a king, not to be the ultimate Judge who would inspire his people and rally them around the Torah, but to be "like all the nations." They asked for a political leader.

The Jewish people had, in effect, thrown in the towel and accepted defeat. The glorious quest for a lasting Torah utopia was over. The goal of an impregnable citadel of the spirit, of all the people joined in a common effort to establish the perfect Kingdom of God on earth, was perceived as out of reach. The people were emotionally and spiritually exhausted, and they did not believe that the old route to salvation could be travelled successfully yet another time. Henceforth, the political fortunes of the country could not be allowed to depend on its spiritual condition. Henceforth, Israel would have to play by the rules of its neighbors, and for that, they would need a political establishment in the form of a monarchy, the prevalent form of government of the time.

The collapse of the national spirit after he had done so much to revive it was a difficult blow for the aging Samuel to absorb. In a prophetic vision, however, God told him not to take this as a personal rejection, for it is "I whom they have rejected as their King." Nevertheless, God told him to accede to their wishes but also to point out to them the full ramifications of their decision.

Samuel tried hard to dissuade the Elders. A political monarchy, he insisted, would bring an end to their cherished personal and tribal freedoms. Their children would be conscripted into national service, and their wealth would be drained by the insatiable demands of the royal court and bureaucracy. In the end, they would regret their decision, but it would be too late.

But the Elders would not be dissuaded, and Samuel bowed to their wishes. After four centuries, the Period of the Judges was finally drawing to a close. It was a time of achievements that would never again be duplicated, but it was also a time of opportunities forever lost.

In 879 b.c.e., Samuel anointed Saul of the tribe of Benjamin as the first king of Israel. The Period of the Kings had begun.

5

The Experiment of the Kings

*Heed the Word of God, O King of Judah
who sits on David's throne, you and your
servants and your people who come within
these gates.*

(Jeremiah 22:1-2)

The appointment of Saul as the first king of Israel represented the last chance for the Jewish people to recapture a semblance of the utopian dream of the early generations. Saul did not personify the ideal of a Jewish king as the ultimate spiritual leader who would guide the people into the messianic era. That role was reserved for the descendants of the tribe of Judah,[1] while Saul was descended from the tribe of Benjamin. Rather, Saul was an interim king whose responsibilities were primarily military and political. The delicate instrument of the spiritual monarchy of Judah was still being kept in reserve.

Four centuries after it began, the experiment of the Judges had ended. The Jewish people were apparently incapable of sustaining for very long a society without a political superstructure, a society in which "every man did as he pleased."[2] Only the moral authority of the great sages exerted national influence, but the history of the Period of the Judges had shown that moral authority alone was an inadequate societal control.

The experiment of the Kings was now about to begin. Henceforth, the Jewish people would travel a different route towards their historical destiny. A conventional monarchy would first be established to solidify the chaotic Jewish society. In the short term, its goal would be to unite the people in revolt against the Philistine occupation. In the long term, its goal would be to curb the Canaanite associations of the weaker elements and thereby initiate a gradual improvement in the overall spiritual condition of the people.

Saul's mission as king, therefore, was not so much to inspire the people as to fulfill the classic functions of a political monarch. He had been chosen to "save My people from the Philistines"[3] by conventional means. Saul was consistently called *melech*, king, but in the context of his appointment, he was designated more specifically as *nagid*, ruler.[4] There are antagonistic connotations in the roots of the word *nagid*, reflecting the adversarial relationship between governor and governed, whereas the roots of *melech* allude to the giving of advice.[5] Saul was appointed to be a *nagid*, to rule and bring order to the anarchic society of ancient Israel, to pave the way for the spiritual monarchy of Judah which would ultimately guide the people into the messianic era. This was the mission of the House of Saul, if it took a generation or a century or a millennium.

In actuality, it took just two years for the House of Saul to collapse. On a personal level, the fall of Saul was a piteous human tragedy. On the national level, it signalled the loss of yet another grand opportunity, another detour on the road to destiny.

At the time of his selection, Saul was considered to be without equal in personal qualities,[6] although there were some who voiced reservations about his ability to lead effectively. He accepted the crown of Israel with reluctance and humility, turning an apparently deaf ear to the grumblings and mutterings of his detractors. But events would prove that he was indeed sensitive to criticism and reproach, that he was a leader who cared too much about the approval of his followers. And that was the fatal flaw that led to his downfall.

Saul's reign began quite auspiciously. He faced his first national crisis immediately after he was crowned, and he responded well. An Ammonite army under King Nachash besieged the city of Yaveish Gilead in Trans-Jordan. The city offered to surrender and pay tribute, but Nachash disdainfully refused to lift the siege unless all the inhabitants plucked out their right eyes. Saul rallied the Jewish forces, crossed the Jordan River and destroyed the Ammonite camp in a well-executed surprise attack at dawn. Saul's popularity rose dramatically after his victory, and in a great national celebration at Gilgal, his monarchy was reaffirmed and acclaimed.

Emboldened by his early successes and his rising popularity, Saul now took on Philistia by ordering the execution of the Philistine governor of the land of Benjamin. In response, the Philistines invaded Israel, massing an enormous army at Michmash. The Jews massed around their new king in Gilgal.

Earlier, Samuel had arranged to bring instructions from God to Saul at Gilgal, before which Saul was to refrain from offering sacrifices in preparation for the battle with the Philistines. But the appointed day of the meeting with the prophet arrived, and the prophet had still not put in an appearance at Gilgal. As the day wore on, the people began to disperse, and Saul became increasingly agitated. Finally, he could not bear to wait any longer, and he proceeded without prophetic counsel. Just then, the prophet arrived.

Saul tried to excuse his actions, but Samuel would have none of it. Saul's impatience and agitation had revealed a deficiency of faith in the power of prophecy.[7] A Jewish king was meant to be the unflinching instrument of God, which Saul apparently was not. Therefore, Samuel informed him, he had forfeited the right to be the founder of a longlasting dynasty.[8] For the time being, however, Saul himself would still be allowed to continue his kingship and accomplish as much as he could in his own lifetime. Israel was at war with Philistia, and Saul was still the commander.

For a while, Saul's fortunes seemed to brighten. Although vastly outnumbered, Saul and his son Jonathan led the Jewish forces to a stunning victory in the ensuing battle at Michmash. The Philistines were routed and driven back behind their own borders. With the Philistine threat in the southwest temporarily neutralized, Saul turned his attention to securing the other borders, scoring successive victories against Moab and Ammon in the east, the Syrian kingdoms in the north and Edom in the south.

After this string of victories, he was visited once again by the prophet Samuel, and once again, he failed to rise to the occasion. This time, his divine instructions were to settle the long-standing account with the kingdom of Amalek, the malevolent nemesis of the Jewish people. Saul was to give no quarter, take no prisoners, seize no plunder. Saul mustered an army of two hundred and ten thousand men and annihilated Amalek, but he violated the divine command by sparing the life of King Agag and by allowing his soldiers to plunder the livestock they considered too valuable to destroy. This time, he was guilty of more than faintheartedness and impatience. This time, he had deliberately disregarded his instructions in order to curry favor with his troops. And as a consequence, as Samuel was later to inform him, God rejected him and decided to give the crown to his betters.

The designated successor, although Saul was not informed of this, was David the son of Jesse of Bethlehem in the land of Judah. The dawn of the eternal House of David, the spiritual monarchy of Judah, had arrived considerably earlier than anticipated.

Samuel himself was greatly dismayed at the turn events had taken, and although he had not tried to intercede for Saul at Gilgal, he now prayed desperately to God that Saul be given a reprieve. The forfeiture of the dynastic potential of the House of Saul had not posed an immediate danger to the Jewish people. Saul was a relatively young man, and there was still enough time for him to satisfy Israel's political needs and thus pave the way for the spiritual monarchy of Judah. But with Saul's kingship aborted at such an early stage, the future of the Jewish people had suddenly become very problematic.

The mission of the House of Saul had been to impose political order on society, to terminate the anarchic tendencies among the weaker elements and reverse the spiritual decline of the people. But this type of inspired leadership requires a special relationship between the people and their king. It is most effective when the people view him with awe as a paragon of Torah knowledge and saintliness far removed from the administrative aspects of government, as a man whose hands are clean, whose heart is pure and whose spirit soars to the heavens.

Had Saul been successful in stabilizing the political situation before his departure, this type of relationship would have been possible. But he had unfortunately failed, causing the spiritual monarchy of Judah to be inaugurated prematurely. The new king would now have to fulfill the additional role of political architect,[9] which would inevitably diminish his effectiveness as spiritual leader. His involvement in the sordid world of political affairs would undoubtedly tarnish the purity of his image in the public perception.

But even worse, there was the very real possibility that he would be corrupted by excessive contact with the apparatus of temporal power. The spiritual monarchy of Judah was a delicate, finely-tuned instrument, and to introduce it in the present chaos would be like using a scalpel for a task that called for an axe.

Nevertheless, in spite of Samuel's pleading, Saul was not reprieved. Yet another experiment had failed. The attempt at an interim political monarchy compatible with the stringent requirements of the Jewish quest for destiny had been thwarted by the frailties of the human character. Saul, who had been considered the finest person in Israel, had been unable to find that perfect balance between being the absolute king of his people and the absolute servant of God. There was no reason to expect that a lesser man would be able to do it better.

For all the risks involved, the role of the servant-king would now be given to the predestined kings of Judah. Perhaps their critical role as spiritual leaders would help them overcome the difficulties of finding the perfect balance that had eluded Saul. The difficulties would be daunting, but in the end, it would be a matter of free will. Perhaps these men of destiny would make the right choices and the drifting ship of the Jewish people would once again return to its destined course.

The first of the kings of Judah, and the greatest, did indeed find that perfect balance between king of his people and the servant of God. David was the ideal Jewish king, a righteous soul bonded with steel chains of love to God and his Torah, drawing his wisdom, his emotions, his courage and his aspirations from the eternal fountainhead of the holy Torah. In the synagogue, he prayed and studied with heart-dissolving fervor. In his audience chamber, he was gentle and compassionate. On the battlefield, he was the fearless instrument of God plunging into battle with weapons of the soul even as his hands wielded an expert sword. David was in love with God and His people, and his love was returned in equal measure.

David was one of the greatest men who ever lived. He appeared at a time when his people had fallen to their lowest point since becoming a nation, when the experiments of the Judges and the interim monarchy had failed and the future looked bleaker than it ever had. In those dark days, David burst upon the scene like a flash of lightning that illuminates Jewish life to this very day. The passionate verses of the Psalms, most of which he composed,[10] reverberate with such intense spiritual yearning and sheer poetic beauty that they have become an inexhaustible source of solace and inspiration throughout the ages. From the pages of the Psalms springs the vivid image of David, the Sweet Singer of Israel,[11] greeting the dawn with the sweet strains of his harp and the sweeter sounds of his words of love for the Creator.

This was the man God chose to sit on the throne of Israel. This was the man whose reign would inaugurate the eternal dynasty of the House of David from which the future Messiah will be descended. This was a man so utterly bonded with God that his kingship would be an extension of the Kingship of God. David was the perfect choice for King of Israel.

In the meantime, however, although David had been anointed secretly by Samuel in Bethlehem, the time for his actual accession to the throne had not yet come. The doomed reign of Saul would first have to play itself out to its tragic end.

As Saul's reign entered its waning days, he began to suffer from bouts of severe melancholia, and he asked for the services of a harp player to ease his mental torment. His advisors recommended David of Bethlehem, a fine musician, a courageous fighter and a man of wisdom. Saul instantly developed a great affection for the young David. He appointed David to the coveted post of royal arms bearer, keeping him constantly by his side. And when Saul fell into one of his black moods, David would play for him and give him some measure of relief.

Meanwhile, the war with Philistia was heating up. The Philistines invaded the lands of Judah, and the Philistine and Jewish armies prepared for battle at Socho. But the battle never materialized. According to the military custom of the time, individual champions would sometimes fight in lieu of the armies, and on this occasion, young David met the dreaded Philistine giant Goliath in single combat. David struck him down with a well-placed stone from his slingshot, and the Philistine army withdrew. Saul then gave David a military command and sent him out into the field, where he conducted one successful campaign after another so that his reputation for valor and prowess soon outstripped that of the king.

Before long, Saul realized he was witnessing the prophecy of Samuel unfold as David's rising star eclipsed his own fading star. Saul's apparently inconsequential misstep in Gilgal had derailed his blossoming career and brought him to the point where he was forced to watch his life unravel before his eyes. The painful clarity of his own downfall was too much for him to endure. He became even more deranged, and during his bouts of melancholia, this former paragon of virtue tried to assassinate his brilliant heir apparent, who remained ever loyal and devoted to his sovereign.

In 877 b.c.e., Samuel passed away, and during the funeral of the venerated prophet, the gathered multitudes were electrified by a sensational disclosure. Samuel's disciples revealed that the prophet had already anointed David as the future king.[12] Afraid that the news would further enrage the disturbed king, David fled to the Paran Desert far to the south, where he stayed for three months until he was again discovered by the king. From there, he went with six hundred followers to the Philistine city of Gath, hopeful that perhaps in Philistia he would finally be beyond the reach of the king.

In Gath, David duped King Achish into believing he was a Jewish renegade ready to side with the Philistines. King Achish granted David's group the outlying town of Tziklag as a place of residence, confident that he had found a loyal ally in his war against the Jewish kingdom. But when the next battle loomed four months later, the distrustful Philistine generals refused to allow David and his men to join them at the front. Thus, David found himself back in Tziklag when the climactic battle was fought at Mount Gilboa.

For the Jews, the battle was a major disaster. The Jewish forces were routed and scattered, and the Philistine armies occupied parts of Trans-Jordan and the Valley of Jezreel. Saul and his son Jonathan were among the numerous battlefield casualties. When the tragic news reached David in Tziklag, he delivered a heartbroken eulogy over the two fallen men; parts of this memorable lament are often quoted in eulogies for great Jewish figures to this very day.

At last, the throne was vacant, but still the House of Saul refused to yield. When David, now thirty years old, returned from Tziklag, he took up residence in Hebron and was acclaimed as king in his native land of Judah. But through the manipulations of Saul's chief minister, the rest of Israel accepted Ish Boshes, Saul's surviving son, as the new king; he was crowned and installed in the strategic city of Machanaim in Trans-Jordan. Thus was the nascent Kingdom of Israel temporarily divided into two separate kingdoms, Judah under David and Israel under Ish Boshes, foreshadowing the future permanent division after the death of Solomon.

For two years, civil war raged, with David's forces steadily gaining the upper hand, until Ish Boshes was assassinated by two members of his own palace guard, bringing the conflict effectively to a close. Nevertheless, five more years passed before David made his triumphal entry into Jerusalem in 869 b.c.e. and was acclaimed as the king of all Israel.[13]

The first foreign reaction to the installation of the House of David in Israel came from King Hiram of the Phoenician city of Tyre. Hiram extended the hand of friendship by sending cedars from the forests of Lebanon along with carpenters and stonemasons to assist in the construction of the royal palace, initiating a long period of cordial relations and close cooperation between Phoenicia and Israel.

Philistia, however, reacted by sending two expeditionary

forces into Israel, both of which were destroyed by David. David then carried the war into the homeland of the Philistines, decisively defeating them and capturing the city of Gath.[14] The last tentacles of Philistine occupation had finally been severed.

After eight long decades, the Philistine War had come to an end. The misery and heartbreak Israel had suffered during this climactic war could finally fade into blessed forgetfulness, but the wrenching changes it had wrought in Jewish society would forever change the course of Jewish history. The old society of the Judges, with all its strengths and deficiencies, no longer existed. A new society stood poised in its place, ready to travel an unknown road to an uncertain future.

For the moment, however, the future would have to wait until the present was safely secured. With Philistia defeated, David turned on the other enemies on the perimeter of Israel. He attacked Moab, making it a tributary vassal of Israel. He defeated King Haddadezer of the Aramean kingdom of Tzovah in Syria, who had been encroaching on the northern borders of Israel. He conquered Damascus in the north and Edom in the south, placing both under the administration of Jewish governors. He then defeated an Ammonite army reinforced by Aramean mercenaries.

Stung by the defeat, the Aramean kingdoms united against Israel. Calling on the support of the Aramean principalities of Mesopotamia, King Haddadezer mustered a large army and penetrated into Trans-Jordan, where David dealt him a crushing blow at Cheilam. In the wake of the defeat, the Aramean kings sued for peace and agreed to pay tribute to Israel. Stripped of its Aramean support, the kingdom of Ammon was isolated, and after a long siege of its capital city, it too fell before the Jewish armies.

Israel had now become a formidable regional power, secure within its borders and feared by its neighbors. The wars were finally over for David, except for several subsequent eruptions of hostilities with Philistia, and his remaining years were occupied by the difficult work of unifying his headstrong people, unaccustomed as they were to being governed by a king. But the healing process had begun, and under the guidance of the determined and courageous king, it continued uninterrupted.

The society remained free of pagan infection, and the spiritual level began to rise once again. The inauguration of the spiritual monarchy of Judah had been a cautious success, but its future prospects were still very much in question.

Towards the end of his life, David purchased a tract of land in Jerusalem for the site of the Holy Temple, which he himself would never see; the task of building a House of God would fall to his successor whose hands had not been stained by the blood of war.[15] In 837 b.c.e., after reigning over a united Israel for thirty-three stormy years, David passed away. He was succeeded by his son Solomon.

In his own way, Solomon was also one of the greatest men who ever lived, but he was not a duplicate of his father David. His father had been a warrior, a passionate and exuberant man who would dance with abandon among the throngs of his people.[16] Solomon, however, was more reserved and restrained, a man more at ease in the cerebral worlds of wisdom than on the heated plains of battle. Pure wisdom was his dominant characteristic and the guiding force of his life.

From the first, Solomon beseeched God for the gift of wisdom, which was granted in such measure that he became "the wisest of all men,"[17] his very name becoming synonymous with wisdom. He studied Torah under the greatest sages of his time and surpassed them in knowledge and understanding. He then explored the frontiers of philosophy and the natural sciences in the light of his vast Torah knowledge, gaining a deeper understanding of the total integration of the physical and spiritual worlds than any man before or after. His almost limitless wisdom, knowledge and poetic vision are impressively displayed in *Proverbs*, *Ecclesiastes* and *The Song of Songs*, the divinely inspired supplementary books of the Torah which he authored.

Solomon's route to popularity with his subjects was also through his phenomenal wisdom, which he used to great advantage in the conduct of his royal duties.[18] Over time, his fame spread far and wide, and nobles came from distant lands to pay homage to him and see for themselves the wonders of his legendary wisdom. He would eventually use his great wisdom to become the master of a far-flung empire without ever waging war or even fighting a single battle, but first he had to build a

House for God in the Jewish capital of Jerusalem.

Solomon's father David, for all his glorious achievements as a warrior and a pacifier, had not been granted the honor and privilege of building a permanent Abode for God in the sacred city of Jerusalem.[19] But Solomon was a man of peace ruling over the pacified land he had inherited from his father. The nation was spiritually purified, secure, prosperous and united behind its wise and illustrious king. After five centuries of temporary residence in the Mishkan in the Desert, Gilgal, Shilo, Nov and Giveon, the time had come to build a permanent residence for the Presence of God to crown this hopeful new society.

In 833 b.c.e., the mammoth construction project began. Covering an entire hilltop at the highest point of the city of Jerusalem, the magnificent complex of structures, courtyards and walls rose over a period of seven years before the dazzled eyes of the people.

The construction of the Holy Temple marked the fulfillment of the Biblical promises to the Jewish people. They had been brought out of bondage in Egypt, given the Torah, given the land, brought to a state of peace, security and prosperity and crowned with the Divine Presence in their midst. At last, they could set their sights on the messianic age which was coming into view on the distant horizon.

The Jewish people had proven incapable of reaching this point by internal fortitude under conditions of total freedom. The attempt at an interim monarchy had also been found wanting. Only the external stimulus of the spiritual monarchy of Judah, held so long in guarded reserve, had brought them to this happy state. During the four golden decades of Solomon's reign, the people lived under ideal conditions, free to study the Torah in security "in the shade of their own grapevines and date palms."[20] There had never been, nor would there ever be, a more propitious time for making the final leap to the highest levels of spiritual achievement attainable by mortal man. The possibility that disaster lurked unnoticed in the shadows was far from anyone's mind. But lurk there it did, waiting for complacency, its old accomplice, to open up the door.

In the meantime, as the spiritual level of the country continued to rise under his wise guidance, Solomon prepared to safeguard the future security and stability of Israel without resorting to war. He chose a two-pronged approach, economic and diplomatic. Both would prove successful in the short term, but the long term was an altogether different matter.

On the economic front, he formed a mercantile alliance with Hiram, the king of the Phoenician city of Tyre, who had befriended David and had subsequently sent gifts to Solomon for the Holy Temple.

The Phoenicians were accomplished sailors, but they had no access to the Red Sea trading routes; the Suez Canal would not be built for another two and a half thousand years. In cooperation with Solomon, they now built a large trading fleet at the port of Etzion Gever near Eilat on the northern arm of the Red Sea. From there, the Phoenician-Jewish fleets sailed to East Africa and brought back immense treasures of gold, silver, coral and ivory, as well as apes and peacocks.[21]

This advantageous alliance also provided the impetus for the Phoenician colonization of the entire Mediterranean basin, around which they built dozens of trading colonies, such as Cadiz in Spain and the metropolis of Carthage in North Africa. The financial strength and strategic location of Israel and the maritime talents of Phoenicia proved a very potent combination, and within a few short years, the Phoenician-Jewish economic axis dominated the markets of the civilized world.

On the diplomatic front, Solomon exploited the growing prestige of his young kingdom to conclude treaties with numerous major and minor powers in the Imperial Quadrant. Under Solomon, Israel had emerged as the foremost power of the Quadrant, eclipsing Egypt and the Amorite kingdoms of Mesopotamia. Israel had a strong army, a huge cavalry and thousands of war chariots. Enormous wealth poured into Jerusalem from tributary payments, internal economic growth and the Phoenician-Jewish mercantile empire. The nations of the Quadrant had witnessed the rise of empires from less auspicious beginnings, and they were afraid Israel would soon embark on a program of regional conquest. With all the imperial weapons at Israel's disposal, and its outstanding strategic location, it was only reasonable to expect Israel to harbor such notions. The opportunity to form alliances with Israel was therefore very appealing to the regional powers in the Quadrant.

In the custom of the times, as indeed the custom remained until the last centuries, diplomatic treaties between two kingdoms were sealed by matrimonial alliances between the respective royal families. And thus, each of the treaties Solomon signed came along with the hand of a royal princess, who was, of course, duly converted to Judaism. The nations stumbled over each other in their eagerness to sign the treaties, sweetening the dowries of their princesses with extravagant gifts; even the mighty Egyptian pharaoh went to the trouble of conquering the Canaanite city of Gezer just to add it to the dowry of the daughter he had given Solomon. By the time all the treaties were signed, Solomon had a thousand wives, a sure invitation to catastrophe.

After such a long string of glorious successes, Solomon's

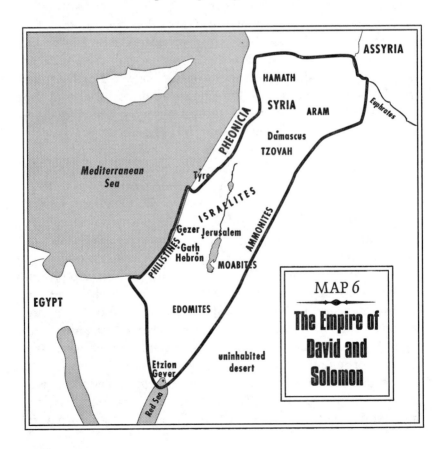

MAP 6

The Empire of David and Solomon

great wisdom had finally led him astray. "Let not the wise man pride himself on his wisdom," the prophet advises,[22] for in the end, a man is but a man. For no mortal man is completely immune to the weakness of the flesh, to minuscule pricks of vanity, to twinges of forgotten pride, to the vulnerability of emotion.

Solomon had reached frontiers of wisdom upon which no other man would ever tread, and as he writes in *Ecclesiastes*, he had penetrated the veneers of all worldly pursuits and found them meaningless. He thus became, as much as a man can be, a being of pure intellect and spirituality, a holy denizen of the celestial worlds. He forgot the vain and confused world of ordinary men, and he forgot that little fragments of that world would be buried in his soul as long as warm blood flowed through his veins.

In its commandments to the king of Israel, the Torah declares, "Let him not marry too many women, so that he not be led astray."[23] Although the Torah generally does not give reasons for its commandments, the Torah had seen fit here to state explicitly that this particular commandment had been given for precautionary purposes. Solomon, therefore, assumed that the interpretation of "too many" was subjective and that each king must ascertain for himself how many women he could safely marry without being led astray.[24] For most men, a thousand wives would most definitely be "too many," but Solomon was infinitely superior to most men. If his diplomatic initiatives for the welfare of Israel required that he marry a thousand princesses, this holy sage believed he could do so with immunity. He was mistaken.

These foreign princesses had all been raised in pagan societies, but now that they had been given in marriage to Solomon, they were indoctrinated in the truths of Torah and converted.[25] Even in the best case, however, it would be difficult for such converts to develop a deep and abiding Jewish identity, and the situation of these princesses was far from a best case scenario. Quite probably, some had never given more than lip service to their new faith, and even the sincere ones were not long removed from the pagan temples of their childhood. Once in Jerusalem, these women were ensconced in opulent palaces and left to their own devices by the generous but preoccupied king. In the absence of a guiding hand and a vigilant eye, the seeds of paganism began to germinate in the royal palace.

Slowly, idols appeared in the royal palace. The sounds of pagan rites and the smells of idolatrous incense began to float through the royal gardens. One after the other, the princesses cast off their outer garments of Judaism and resumed their former identities. Eventually, even some of the more sincere converts began to slide into their old ways. The royal palace of Jerusalem, home of God's anointed king, had now become home as well to hordes of strange gods from numerous lands.

All this happened while Solomon was distracted by his incessant quest for truth and wisdom. He should have seen it coming and stopped it before it was too late, but he paid no attention to the warning signs. The Talmud relates that when Solomon married the Egyptian princess she showed him musical instruments and told him how they were used in the pagan rites. Solomon, however, did not reprimand her for speaking of her pagan past. He just let the remarks pass without comment.[26]

At best, we can only speculate about the reasons for Solomon's silence and tender indulgence. Perhaps he thought she was teasing him and decided not to respond. Perhaps he thought she was making small talk and that these things were really no longer important to her. Perhaps he sensed the strains of her cultural adjustment and decided not to make an issue of it, hoping that with time such nostalgic thoughts would fade from her mind. Whatever his reason, he surely did not suspect that she was an insincere convert.

Yet he should have suspected. He should have been vigilant and critical. He should have discerned the perfidy of his foreign wives and the hollowness of their professed faith. He should have foreseen the problems and nipped them in the bud. But he did not, and by his negligent silence, he allowed his kingdom to be contaminated and eventually destroyed.

"When Solomon grew old, his wives persuaded him to follow alien gods," the prophet Jeremiah wrote in *The Book of Kings* four centuries later, "and he was not as loyal to God his Lord as was his father David . . . Then Solomon built an altar to Khemosh, the abomination of Moab, on the mountain facing Jerusalem, and to Molech, the abomination of Ammon. And he did the same for all his foreign wives who burned incense and sacrificed to their gods."[27]

It is absurd to think that Solomon, the wise and holy prophet, suddenly became an old fool, a depraved idol worshipper building altars for the gods of all his foreign wives. In actuality, he did none of these things, as the Talmud explains, but because he was silent, he bears the blame for all the abominations of his wives.[28]

Jeremiah was not writing history but ethical instruction, and we must read between the lines to glean historical information. These words were said to shock, like a parent who exaggerates the crime of a child to emphasize its gravity. Yet even in the midst of this intense criticism, the prophet lets fall a hint that this is not actual fact by saying that Solomon "was not as loyal as his father David." Solomon was undoubtedly loyal to God, the Talmud infers from this, but not quite with the perfect loyalty of David. David would never have allowed something like this to happen right under his nose, but Solomon did.

The spiritual monarchy of Judah had been contaminated beyond repair, and the citadel of Israel had been breached, not from the weakest elements this time but from the very top. The royal princes were children of idolatrous mothers, and the holy air of Jerusalem smarted with the stench of pagan rites. Therefore, God informed Solomon, the kingship would be taken away from the House of David. For the sake of the loyal David, however, Solomon would be allowed to live out his days as king of a united Israel, but after his death, his descendants would reign only over the tribe of Judah.

How quickly the mighty had fallen! Just a few short years before, the Jewish people had stood at the pinnacle of their history, secure, prosperous, inspired, forging ahead towards the messianic age which beckoned from the horizon. But it had all been a mirage. All that beckoned now was the gaping maw of a dark tunnel whose end was nowhere in sight.

What had caused this terrible downfall? Certainly, Solomon's negligent silence was the direct cause. But was Solomon the only one who was silent? What of all the other people in the royal palace and in the rest of Jerusalem? And how did these foreign women dare trample on the sacred values of their adopted country? Surely, not all the people were wandering in the stellar reaches of wisdom, too distracted to notice the abominations around them. Surely, a thousand royal princesses performing pagan rites must have left some telltale bits of evidence. Surely, there must have been some rumors, some whispered gossip about scandal in the royal palace. Why was there no hue and cry? Why didn't the people rise up and storm the gates of the palace? Why didn't they demand that Solomon control his wives?

Clearly, something was fundamentally wrong with Jewish society. Clearly, the pagan influences of the Philistine days were buried but not dead. Clearly, the new piety and purity were only surface deep, and underneath, the polluted society of yesteryear was still fresh in the collective memory. The activities of the foreign princesses did not shock the people, and if Solomon did not bother to protest, they did not feel compelled to do so either. But indifference is a form of acceptance, and by their averted eyes, the Jewish people had condoned the idolatry in the royal palace. Solomon may have been guilty of negligent silence, but they were guilty of deliberate silence.

The prophet Samuel's nightmare had become reality. The spiritual monarchy of Judah had been introduced before its time, and the people had not risen to the challenge. The purification of society had not been deep enough, and now, this delicate and precious instrument had been blunted and disfigured. What hope was left for the Jewish people? How would they recapture the spiritual exaltation of the early generations? And even if they somehow could, who would lead them across the final hurdles into the messianic age?

In a sense, this is the most tragic point in Jewish history. With the benefit of hindsight, we can see the future of the Jewish people stretching away from this point in a seemingly endless trail across the desolate expanses of time, sometimes rising, sometimes falling, but never again with a clear view of the ultimate destination.

We see the kingdom torn asunder. We see the permanent demise of the northern half of the kingdom and the temporary demise of the southern half. We see ever stronger alien attacks on the embattled Jewish people. We see the breaches and the hemorrhage and the tragedy of exile. And throughout the ages, we see the core element of the Jewish people, ever steadfast, ever faithful, standing arm in arm around the holy Torah to form a human citadel; we see these tragic heroes endlessly struggling, persistently hopeful, desperately trying to fend off the destroyer and rebuild a lost world from the indestructible kernel that remains.

From this point on, we see the Jewish people become like the mountain climber who, slipping and sliding, scrapes and scrabbles his way up the mountainside only to slide back to the bottom just before he reaches the top. From this point on, the dogged climb goes on, but the slipping and sliding takes place much closer to the base of the mountain. From this point on, although freedom of choice is never restricted, there is little hope of meeting destiny through a monolithic national effort and a triumphant entry into the messianic era. There is only hope that the indestructible, incorruptible core element, no matter how shrunken in size, will bring on the messianic age through an outcry of anguished prayer, that God in His infinite compassion will reach down and lift His tormented children to the mountaintop that has always eluded them.

According to Jewish belief, the fortunes of the offspring of Jacob and the offspring of Esau are in constant counterbalance to each other; when the one falls, the other rises.[29] Until the reign of Solomon, the course of Jewish history, for all its fitful lurches, had followed a rising imperative, probing one method after another to reach the shining goal of its destiny. But now, all methods were exhausted, all methods had failed, and the historical imperative shifted to the other side.

The Talmud exclaims that when Solomon married the Egyptian pharaoh's daughter the angel Gabriel went down and drove a reed into the Mediterranean Sea and upon this reed the great city of Rome arose; the early stirrings of Roman power coincide with the reign of Solomon.[30]

At this point, when the last grand opportunity of Jewish history was missed, the Roman descendants of Esau began their long and gradual ascent to temporal power, and the Jewish people began their long and gradual descent from temporal power. The first cracks appeared towards the end of Solomon's reign with the insurrection of the Syrian dominions. Although it would not be completed for several centuries, the disintegration of the Jewish kingdom had already begun.

6

Kingdoms in Decline

*The land was filled with idols; they bowed
down to their own handiwork, to what
their fingers had wrought.*

(Isaiah 2:8)

n 797 b.c.e., Solomon was succeeded by his son Rechavam,
but Rechavam did not possess a fraction of his father's
wisdom. When the northern tribes gathered for the coronation ceremony in Shechem,[1] they demanded that Rechavam
ease the tax burden imposed by Solomon. The counsellors who
had served Solomon advised Rechavam to be prudent and
conciliatory, but his hotheaded young friends urged him to
assert his authority and take a militant stance. Rechavam followed the advice of his friends and lost his kingdom. The ten
northern tribes revolted, and after a narrow escape, Rechavam
returned to Jerusalem. The scheduled coronation never took
place.

Israel now split into two separate entities, the Kingdom of
Judah in the south, comprised of the tribes of Judah and Benjamin, with its capital at Jerusalem, and the Kingdom of Israel in
the north, with its capital at Shechem. Rechavam was crowned
as king of Judah in Jerusalem. The Kingdom of Israel chose

97

Yeravam ben Nevat of the tribe of Ephraim as its first monarch.

Yeravam ben Nevat, a brilliant scholar and a capable manager, was eminently suited for the responsibilities that come along with a royal crown. He was the foremost Torah sage of his time,[2] and he had also served under Solomon as the royal administrator of the tribes of Ephraim and Menashe.[3] After the debacle of Solomon's wives, the prophet Achiah of Shilo had informed Yeravam that he would become the *nagid*[4] of the northern tribes, and now, the prophecy had come true.

Once again, we encounter the term *nagid*, as we did with regard to Saul, indicating that Yeravam's mission was also essentially political rather than religious. Clearly, the spiritual monarchy of Judah was being withdrawn from Israel. Henceforth, the country would be governed by a system of conventional monarchy, with the descendant of David in the Kingdom of Judah and the distinguished Yeravam ben Nevat in the Kingdom of Israel.

MAP 7

The Division of the Kingdom

TZOVAH

Dan

PHEONICIA

Samaria • Tirzah   Ramoth Gilead

• Shechem

ISRAEL

Medterranean Sea

Bethel

AMMONITES

Jerusalem

JUDAH

MOABITES

PHILISTIA

EDOMITES

Israel had undoubtedly taken a giant step backward; it had slipped from its proximity to the pinnacle of the mountain. But the division of the kingdom was still a new beginning, albeit on a much lower level. The utopian experiment of the Judges had not succeeded. The transitional monarchy of Saul had not succeeded. The spiritual monarchy of Judah had also been less than successful. It was now time to go back to the drawing board for a new attempt with less ambitious expectations. Now it was time to try a conventional monarchy with no immediate higher goals other than to stabilize and decontaminate Jewish society. Once these goals were accomplished, higher goals would be set, and avenues of approach would be chosen. Perhaps at that time there would be an attempt to travel one of the old avenues once again, or perhaps a new avenue would appear. In the meantime, the focus would be on the present.

For all intents and purposes, the fortunes of the Jewish people were now placed in the capable hands of Yeravam ben Nevat. What followed is one of the most baffling episodes in Biblical history.

As was to be expected from a good administrator, the first order of business for Yeravam as king was to transform the provincial city of Shechem into a national capital. He built a royal palace, expanded the municipal boundaries and strengthened the fortifications. Having attended to the present, his thoughts turned to the future, and he began to brood.

Just a short distance away stood golden Jerusalem with its magnificent Holy Temple to which all Jews made pilgrimages thrice yearly, during the major festivals. Since sitting was forbidden in the Courtyard of the Temple to all but the Davidic kings, the pilgrims from the northern tribes would see Rechavam honored by being allowed to sit and Yeravam demeaned by being required to stand, and they might even begin to have second thoughts about their mutiny. Perhaps they would regret the decision made in anger and yearn to be reconciled with the glorious House of David.[5] Before long, the northern kingdom might disintegrate, and that would be the end of Yeravam's royal pretensions, if not his very life.

Yeravam's shocking solution to this problem set off a chain of events that ultimately brought about the destruction of both the Kingdom of Israel and the Kingdom of Judah. He closed the border between Israel and Judah to all pilgrims, and he built two substitute temples, one in Bethel, the other in Dan. In each of these temples he placed a golden calf, and he declared to the people, "This is the Lord who brought you forth from the land of Egypt!" He then appointed a priestly caste not of Levite descent, and he established new dates for the festivals.

To be sure, Yeravam originally presented these images as symbols for God. He needed to provide his people with a viable alternative to the Holy Temple in Jerusalem, yet he knew he lacked the resources to build temples of equal splendor and magnificence in his own kingdom.[6] Therefore, he decided to offer in his temples something not found in the Holy Temple, an anthropomorphic fertility symbol for the Creator of the Universe.

Whatever his motivation may have been, his actions were in direct violation of numerous Torah commandments and totally inexcusable. Moreover, it is incredible that a man of such greatness in learning could even contemplate a course of action which made a mockery of a lifetime devoted to acquiring a vast knowledge of the Torah.

How could a man like Yeravam ben Nevat have done such a thing? How could he abandon all his convictions and beliefs and forfeit all the spiritual rewards he had painstakingly accumulated through years of toil and sweat? What could have been in his mind?

These questions beggar any answers one might venture to give; there is no rational explanation for Yeravam's crimes. Yet if we stop and contemplate this enigma named Yeravam ben Nevat, we catch a terrifying glimpse of the dark catacombs that lie hidden deep in the human soul. What monsters lurk in those fetid depths! Yeravam had been thrust up to a level about which ordinary humans do not even dream. He had been made a king, and a monster of arrogance escaped from the dark caverns of his soul and swallowed up the whole man, his convictions, his humanity, his future and his past.[7] All we can say is that the man who committed these abominations was not the same man who was chosen to be king.[8]

The effect of the golden calves on Israel was devastating.

The presentation of an anthropomorphic symbol for God undermined the entire Jewish concept of divinity. Abraham had rebelled against the notion of a god race, of deities as supernatural creatures, vastly superior to man but restricted nonetheless. He had declared to the world that God was totally spiritual, above space and time, unbound by any restrictions, indefinable and unknowable. How could such a God be represented by an image? Wasn't it a contradiction in terms?

And thus, as the northern tribes began to frequent the new temples in Bethel and Dan, their conception of God deteriorated. As time passed, they came to see Him as their own champion among the deities of the god race. They revered His Torah and obeyed His laws, but they did not know Him. They thought of Him as something He is not, something infinitely inferior to what He really is. In this frame of mind, the practice of Judaism became a form of idolatry, for they were worshipping a deity that did not exist in reality. The great Yeravam ben Nevat had launched the Kingdom of Israel by forcing idolatry upon his subjects.

In the Kingdom of Judah, things were also going less than splendidly. Rechavam's first impulse had been to attempt to suppress the rebellion by force, but he desisted when told by the prophet Shemeiah that God wanted the kingdom divided; a protracted civil war did break out, however, between the two sister kingdoms when Rechavam's son Aviam came of age.[9] Rechavam then embarked on a major campaign to consolidate his power in the remainder of his realm. He built fortress cities surrounded by moats[10] and stocked them with provisions of food and drink and stockpiles of weapons. At the same time, the best elements from the northern kingdom were streaming into Judah to escape the sacrilegious decrees of Yeravam, further strengthening the southern kingdom.[11]

For three years, this state of affairs continued, until Rechavam felt that his power base was secured. Then, in the words of the Prophets, "he abandoned the Torah, together with the rest of the Jews,"[12] and he transgressed by "not conditioning himself to seek God."[13] The people of Judah also "angered God" exceedingly by the erection of private altars and monuments and the spread of promiscuous behavior throughout the land.[14] Once again, we must try to penetrate the opaque prose of the Prophets, as we did with the account of Solomon, and distinguish actual events from hyperbole for the purpose of sharp rebuke.

Fate had thrust Rechavam onto the throne of Judah, but he was inadequately equipped for the role. In his veins flowed the blood of David and Solomon, but also the blood of his mother, the Ammonite princess Naamah.[15] Naamah was a good and loyal woman, one of the few of Solomon's wives who remained true to her adopted faith.[16] It had taken great courage and determination for her to resist the frenzy of recidivist paganism around her without the support of her distracted husband, and she applied this same courage and determination to the upbringing of her son Rechavam. Unfortunately, however, she could not give Rechavam more than she herself possessed, and her own conceptions of Judaism were deficient in many respects.

Naamah was a child of her times. Raised in the pagan society of the Kingdom of Ammon, she grew up with a conception of divinity based on the prevalent notions of the god race. When she married Solomon, she willingly accepted her husband's religion, as princesses given in marriage customarily did, and she converted to Judaism. But we can safely assume that, in her mind, all Judaism did was narrow the field of the god race, so that instead of there being many members to the god race there was only one.

In her mind, there was no direct metaphysical bond between God and the Jews, just as there was no direct bond between the Ammonites and their gods. She understood that the Jews owed Him their loyalty and obedience, but once they had fulfilled their obligations, she believed they were free to pursue their independent lives. She could not fathom that the entire life of the Jew is his striving to consummate his relationship with God and achieve perfect union with Him, that the Torah is his very lifeblood. This idea was so alien to Naamah, transplanted child of the pagan world, that it would have taken years of intense acculturation for it to penetrate beyond a surface acknowledgment. But Naamah did not receive this kind of indoctrination. Instead, she was exposed to the influences of all the numerous wives who were backsliding into the paganism they had once left behind.

Naamah meant well, and considering her situation, she probably achieved much more than could be expected. But in the final analysis, her view of Judaism was constricted by her residual pagan attitudes. She did not understand the role of the Torah beyond its function as a code of law, and she did not understand that a Jew must "seek God" in every aspect of his life.

Rechavam, as the son of Solomon, undoubtedly received the best Torah education possible, but it was inevitable that he would also be influenced by the attitudes of his virtuous mother. His loyalty to God and the Torah must surely have been reinforced by Naamah's participation in his upbringing, but at the same time, his conception of God and the Torah were weakened by it.

Therefore, as long as Rechavam was building defenses for Judah to protect the Torah life that flourished within it, his mind was filled with thoughts of the Torah and its importance to the Jewish people. But once the fortifications were complete and the land secured, the role of the Torah in his life receded. He had dutifully fulfilled his obligations to God and His Torah, and now, he could give some thought to his own independent life. And thus, in the angry words of the Prophet, he "abandoned the Torah" and did not "condition himself to seek God." It would seem that Rechavam did not truly comprehend that the Jewish people, the Torah and God were indivisible.

As Rechavam's primary interests shifted from the Torah to other pursuits, there was a ripple effect of apathy throughout society. Cracks in the spiritual fabric of the kingdom began to appear as the people turned inward and became self-indulgent, and there was a pronounced relaxation of moral strictures, which led to promiscuous behavior. It was a new experience for the Jewish people.

Previously, promiscuous behavior among the weaker elements of Jewish society was associated only with the periodic lapses into paganism during the times of the Judges. Promiscuity among nominally loyal Jews was simply nonexistent. The glue of Jewish society during the Period of the Judges had been adherence to the Torah, and therefore, serious transgression had social as well as spiritual consequences. A Jew could not flaunt the Torah in public and still be considered a stalwart member of society; only those who abandoned Jewish society by frequenting the Canaanite temples could even contemplate promiscuity.

However, once society was reorganized along more conventional lines, one could maintain a Jewish identity merely by national citizenship, regardless of one's level of Torah observance. Therefore, the national level of observance depended on the tone set by the government. Saul, David and Solomon had been in the forefront of the national drive for spiritual growth. The people knew that Torah was the air their kings breathed and that the resources of government were all directed towards the furtherance of Torah among the people. In such circumstances, one could clearly not separate observance from citizenship. But under Rechavam, the fire of Torah was lacking in the government, because it was lacking in the king. The people sensed this and no longer felt that their Jewish identity would suffer from a little laxity in Torah observance. Meticulous observance became a matter of personal preference, and among the less meticulous, promiscuity was the result.

The decline in the spiritual condition of Judah was further exacerbated by the example of neighboring Israel. It resulted in a direct affront to the Almighty by the widespread desecration of the sacrificial service.

In Joshua's times, the portable Mishkan in Gilgal had been considered an itinerant residence for the Divine Presence, and thus, individual Jews had been permitted to bring sacrificial offerings on private altars. After the Mishkan was installed in a stone structure in Shilo, however, private altars were prohibited; with the Divine Presence in fixed residence, the *mechitzos*, the sanctified boundaries, were established, and everything outside was considered *chutz*, beyond the pale.

The Presence of God is, of course, ubiquitous in the world, but there is a *tzimtzum*, a veiling and constriction of the Divine Energy, so to speak, in order to allow the physical world to exist. During the Giving of the Torah at Mount Sinai, the veil was pulled aside for a brief moment, and the world trembled almost to the point of disintegration. In the Mishkan, however, only a corner of the veil was lifted, and this partial reversal of the *tzimtzum* created a supremely sanctified island of pure spirituality in the physical world. In the itinerant Mishkan of Gilgal only a small corner of the veil was lifted, and thus, its level of holiness did not generate sanctified boundaries. But in the Mishkan of Shilo, there was a greater emanation of Divine Energy, generating boundaries beyond which the sacred service was forbidden.

After Shilo was destroyed in the days of Samuel, the Mishkan again returned to an itinerant state in Gilgal, Nov and Giveon successively, and private altars were again permitted. But once the Holy Temple was built in Jerusalem, it became the eternal permanent residence of the Divine Presence, and private altars were forever prohibited.[17] The Holy Temple became a permanent bridge between the physical world and the world of pure spirit, the place where a person stood in the Presence of God to a degree impossible anywhere else in the universe. This was where the sacrificial service was to be performed according to the Torah, and to spurn the Presence of God and perform the service elsewhere was considered a transgression in the class of *chaivei kerisos*, one of the most serious in the Torah.

Under Rechavam, however, this was exactly what happened in Judah, not in isolated cases but on a national scale. The people of Judah saw the great convenience their cousins in Israel enjoyed by the availability of the substitute temples in Bethel and Dan, and a significant number of them sought this same convenience for themselves. In their debilitated spiritual state, they had begun to view their periodic visits to the Temple as burdensome obligations rather than exhilarating opportunities to stand in the Presence of God, and they began to sacrifice on private altars to avoid the bother and expense of visiting the Temple. Although this was expressly forbidden by the Torah, they rationalized that if the learned Yeravam ben Nevat had discovered some legal justification for the practice in the northern kingdom it surely applied to the southern kingdom as well.[18]

From our vantage point, it is impossible to determine the extent of the twin erosions of promiscuity and the desecration of the sacrificial service, but we cannot help experiencing a feeling of *deja vu*. During the Period of the Judges, the elite of the people had also suffered from the consequences of the decline of the weaker elements, and now, once again, the entire country was jeopardized by the spiritual decline. But the lessons of history were being ignored. Regardless of the number of righteous people, and there were undoubtedly many, the spiritual fabric of the collective society of the Kingdom of Judah was beginning to disintegrate.

For the remainder of the reign of Rechavam and the entire reign of his son Aviam, there was basically no change in the situation in Judah. But in 777 b.c.e., Aviam's son Asa ascended to the throne, and for a brief while, it seemed as if the downward trend would be arrested and reversed.

Asa was a king in the mold of David and Solomon, intensely loyal and consummately devoted to God. During the forty-one years of his reign, this fiery king struggled to repair the breaches to the citadel of Judaism. He destroyed all the idols brought in by Solomon's foreign wives, and he divested all the royal ladies of foreign descent, including his own grandmother, of all power and influence in the royal palace. He also campaigned vigorously against the disgraceful promiscuity which had defiled his people and virtually eliminated it.[19] Asa taught the Kingdom of Judah "to seek God,"[20] but try as he did, he was unable to break the widespread habit of sacrificing on private altars.[21]

Towards the end of his reign, Asa made a political decision whose catastrophic consequences would not become manifest for two generations. In 749 b.c.e., he agreed to the marriage of his son Yehoshafat to the daughter of Amri, one of the pretenders to the throne of Israel.

Lacking the inherent political stability of the Davidic dynasty, the Kingdom of Israel had deteriorated badly after its first half century of independence. Yeravam ben Nevat had been succeeded by his son Nadav, who was cut from the same cloth. In 774 b.c.e., Nadav was assassinated during a revolt led by Baasha of the tribe of Issachar.[22] Baasha wiped out the entire House of Yeravam and moved the capital to Tirzah. Baasha then laid heavy siege to Jerusalem, and Asa was only able to break the siege by bribing Ben-haddad, the Syrian king, to attack Baasha in the north. Internally, Baasha was as corrupt as Yeravam and Nadav, and when he died in 751 b.c.e., he was replaced by his son Eilah, who was not any better.

In 750 b.c.e., Eilah was assassinated by one of his chariot commanders named Zimri, who then seized the throne and wiped out the entire House of Baasha. But his reign lasted a mere seven days. The military crowned Amri, the commander-in-chief of the armed forces, and in the brief civil war that ensued, Zimri perished. But Amri's claim to the throne was still not undisputed. Although the military supported the candidacy of Amri, there was considerable popular support for a civilian candidate named Tivni ben Ginas.

At this point, Asa decided to interfere in the internal politics of the Kingdom of Israel. Civil war had raged between the two sister kingdoms for many years, and Asa had suffered through the siege of Jerusalem by Baasha. The political turmoil following the death of Zimri now presented him with an opportunity to gain some control over the breakaway kingdom. By throwing his support to one of the pretenders, he could bring an end to the civil war and gain an influential voice in the new government. He decided to take the plunge and accepted Amri's daughter in marriage to his son Yehoshafat. After five long years of strife, the support of Asa helped Amri consolidate his hold on the throne and the kingdom.[23]

The civil war did indeed come to an end, as Asa had hoped, but he had miscalculated badly. By forming a marriage bond with Amri, Asa had exposed the renascent Davidic dynasty to the endemic instability and corrosive influences of the royal houses of Israel. In the long term, this exposure would bring about the destruction of his kingdom.

As it turned out, Amri was worse than any of the kings who preceded him, but his reign was relatively short. After gaining undisputed control of the kingdom, he built a new royal capital in Shomron, where he reigned for six more years. In 739 b.c.e., he died and was succeeded by his son Ahab.

As a king, Ahab was a capable commander and politician, but as a Jew, he was a total disaster. He travelled to the Phoenician city of Sidon and chose as his wife a princess named Jezebel, a faithful adherent of the Baal cult. Jezebel was a thoroughly pagan woman, and it is unlikely that she converted to Judaism[24]; Ahab probably did not demand a conversion, and even if he had, it only would have been *pro forma* and therefore invalid. While still in Sidon, Jezebel introduced Ahab to the worship of the Baal, and upon their return to Israel, Ahab built a temple for the Baal in the royal capital of Shomron, where he worshipped regularly.[25]

The abominations of Yeravam had finally played themselves out to their logical conclusion. By installing anthropomorphic symbols for God in the substitute temples in Bethel and Dan, Yeravam had blurred the Jewish conception of God, and as the years went by, the people were hard pressed to differentiate between the God of Israel and the imaginary deities of the god race. Presently, the people of the northern kingdom began to adopt the tolerant pagan attitude towards foreign deities. As long as their neighbors didn't interfere with the native religion, the people felt, what was wrong with respecting the religious beliefs of others? After all, there was plenty of room in the pantheon for other people's gods.

Clearly, it was only a matter of time before the people would begin to experiment with some of the more popular alien cults. The situation was now far worse than it had been during the Period of the Judges. In those times, Judaism had been internally strong, and the outbreaks of paganism had been caused by waning zeal and lack of societal control among the weaker elements. In the northern kingdom, however, the entire Jewish religion had been corrupted by its kings, and the slide towards paganism resulted from the virtual demise of true Judaism in the north.

Still, although the religion of the north had deteriorated to the point where it was not much different from the pagan cults, it continued to bear a surface resemblance to authentic Judaism. The people continued to live by the laws and ethics of the Torah, but they did not appreciate the spirit and the ideals of the Torah; they did not "seek God." As long as this tenuous connection existed, however, there was hope for a turnaround. Perhaps someday there would be an awakening and the people would discover the true meaning of the life they had been living by habitual rote. But until then, it would take only one breach in the fragile barriers and the kingdom of Israel would be inundated in a pagan deluge. The bold and arrogant young Ahab, child of his times, built a temple to the Baal in Shomron and provided the final breach that devastated the Kingdom of Israel.

Under Ahab and Jezebel, Israel was converted to a polytheistic society in the prevalent mold of the ancient world, to the point that there remained only seven thousand Jews who had never acknowledged the Baal.[26] The Torah was still the law of the land, but the Jewish concept of the unknowable, timeless, totally spiritual God was all but forgotten. Jezebel would not tolerate intolerance, and she slaughtered most of the Jewish prophets who preached the exclusivity of the God of Israel. The God of Israel, in the new popular view promulgated by Ahab and Jezebel, was no more than another of the deities of the god race, albeit a powerful one, and in the spirit of tolerance, it was only fair and hospitable that homage be paid to the ancestral gods of the queen as well.

Throughout his reign, Ahab carried this polytheistic outlook as an armor against the undeniable power of the Jewish prophets. When the prophet Elijah bested the prophets of the Baal in a spectacular public contest on Mount Carmel, Ahab did not lose faith in the Baal. When Ben-haddad, the Syrian king, besieged Shomron, the prophet Michaihu ben Yimlah informed Ahab of the exact details of his deliverance,[27] but still, Ahab was not moved. When Ben-haddad returned the following year and the prophet again predicted his defeat, Ahab was still unmoved. Only Elijah's dire prophecy of the violent end of his royal house gave Ahab pause and struck fear into his heart. But three years later, when the war with Syria resumed, we find him again seeking the advice of the prophets of the Baal. Ahab acknowledged the awesome might of the God of Israel, but he did not acknowledge His exclusivity.

For twenty-two years, Ahab ravaged the sanctified foundations of Jewish society in his own kingdom, and he also managed to drag down neighboring Judah, which was ruled by his righteous brother-in-law Yehoshafat, the son of Asa. Under Ahab, the developing bond between the two sister kingdoms was carefully cultivated. The detente initiated by Amri and Asa was solidified by an informal military alliance and the marriage of Yehoshafat's oldest son Yehoram to Ahab's daughter Asaliah.[28] Yehoram, the crown prince of Judah, was thus Ahab's son-in-law as well as his nephew. The poisons of the House of Ahab[29] had been injected into Judah. It would not take long for the symptoms to appear.

In 717 b.c.e., Ahab was killed on the battlefield while trying to recapture Ramoth Gilead from Syria. He was succeeded by his son Achaziah who was as enthusiastic a worshipper of the Baal as was his father. Two years later, Achaziah died and was succeeded by his brother Yehoram. Yehoram was a slight improvement over his forebears. He himself did not worship the Baal, but neither did he interfere with his mother Jezebel's promotion of the Baal cult in the Jewish kingdom. He also did not remove the golden calves which Yeravam had installed in Bethel and Dan.

In the meantime, Yehoram's cousin by the same name had succeeded to the throne of Judah in 711 b.c.e., after which he slaughtered all the other sons of his father Yehoshafat. Yehoram of Judah turned out to be a truer scion of the House of Ahab than Yehoram of Israel. For all its problems, Judah had not suffered widespread idolatry among the general population, but under Yehoram of the bloodstained hands, a temple of the Baal was erected in Jerusalem.[30] Yehoram of Judah reigned for eight years and was succeeded by his son Achaziah, who followed in the exact footsteps of his father.

The House of Ahab had brought the Jewish people to the lowest point in their history. Less than a century after the golden era of Solomon, there was hardly a trace left of the former glory of ancient Israel. The noble kingdom built on the highest ideals of mankind was but the palest shadow of its former self.

Deprived of the special favor of God, the Jewish nation tumbled from its former position of dominance in the Imperial Quadrant and was replaced by the rising power of the Syrians and the Babylonians. Economic cooperation with the Phoenician cities dwindled after the partition. Periodic raids and extortions depleted the national treasuries. Moab rebelled against Israel during the reign of Achaziah, and Edom rebelled against Judah during the reign of Yehoram. In the north, there was constant war with Syria. In the south, Egypt continued to exert hostile pressure. And far to the northeast, the new colossus of Assyria was beginning to flex its muscles and turn its avaricious eyes towards the Mediterranean coastal lands. The future did not bode well for ancient Israel.

In 702 b.c.e., the prophet Elisha sent an emissary to Jehu, one of the generals of the army of Israel, to anoint him as the new king of Israel and enjoin him to destroy the House of Ahab. With the support of his fellow officers, Jehu organized a revolt and assumed the reins of power.

The accession of Jehu to the throne of Israel was the last real hope for the troubled country. Jehu was not a self-appointed pretender to the throne but the anointed messenger of God sent to redeem the northern kingdom. True to his divine mission, Jehu executed Yehoram and the entire House of Ahab, as well as Achaziah, the corrupt king of Judah, who was visiting his cousin Yehoram. He then eradicated the Baal cult from the Kingdom of Israel and executed all the worshippers of the Baal. But that was where he stopped. He did not destroy the sacrilegious temples Yeravam had erected in Bethel and Dan, the root of all the evil, because he feared a resumption of pilgrimages to Jerusalem might lead to reunification and the loss of his crown.[31] In the end, his personal ambition caused him to fail and the last hope for Israel to be dashed.

Ironically, the final drama of the doomed House of Ahab played itself out in the Kingdom of Judah. After the death of Achaziah, his mother Asaliah exterminated all the heirs to the throne and seized it for herself; as her husband Yehoram had killed all his brothers, she now killed all her grandchildren. Only her one-year-old grandchild Yoash survived in a hiding place in the Temple. For six years, this evil daughter of Ahab sat on the throne of the Davidic kings and ruled the Kingdom of Judah. In the seventh year, the seven-year-old Yoash was brought out of hiding and crowned, triggering a popular uprising. Asaliah was executed, and the temple of the Baal was destroyed.

In Israel, the House of Jehu, which had begun with such hope, delivered fully a century of political stability, but it did little to divert the northern kingdom from its collision course with disaster. Jehu's son Yehoachaz was generally ineffective, but his grandson Yoash, who had a close relationship with the prophet Elisha, was more successful in the endless Syrian wars. In 647 b.c.e., Yoash was succeeded by Yeravam II, who reigned for forty years. This second Yeravam made significant military and economic gains, but he also brought about the ruination of Israel. Baal worship returned with a vengeance, along with the most virulent forms of pagan immorality. Dishonesty, exploitation, promiscuity and all the other fine qualities of self-centered pagan societies in the grand Canaanite tradition of Sodom and Gomorrah took hold in Israel.

In 607 b.c.e., Yeravam II was succeeded by his son Zechariah who reigned for six short months before he was assassinated and replaced by Shalum, who was himself assassinated and replaced one month later by Menachem ben Gadi. Thus ended the tenure of the House of Jehu and the dreams of the tribes who had come to this land with a vision of creating a utopia in which to live by the Torah and seek God, an oasis of holiness in the vast pagan desert of the ancient world.

The die was cast. The Kingdom of Israel had turned away from God. It had become no different from the other pagan countries of its time, and there was no reason why it should be spared a similar fate as well. The special divine protection which keeps the Jewish people from being swallowed up in the quicksands of history was now withdrawn from that segment known as the Kingdom of Israel.

The distant thunder of the ascendant Assyrian power began to draw closer. In the days of Yeravam II, as Israel was sinking into the pit of depravity, the prophet Jonah had carried a message of God to the Assyrian capital of Nineveh to condemn its thievery and injustice. The message of the God of the Jews was received with humility and repentance, in stark contrast to the attitudes of the Jews themselves who continued to ignore the warnings of their own prophets such as Hosheia and Amos. And thus the star of Assyria waxed as the star of Israel waned.

Shortly after Menachem ben Gadi mounted the throne, Israel was invaded by a large Assyrian force. After extorting an enormous payment, the Assyrians withdrew, but the looming shadow of the conquerors lingered long after they left. In 597 b.c.e., Menachem was succeeded by his son Pekachiah, who was assassinated and replaced two years later by Pekach ben Remaliah, one of his generals. Pekach ben Remaliah formed an alliance with Syria, his erstwhile enemy, against the common threat of Assyria, but it was to no avail. Under King Tiglath-Pileser, Assyria devoured all of Syria and large chunks of Israel, plundering the country and making it a tributary vassal.

In 574 b.c.e., Hosheia ben Eilah assassinated Pekach ben Remaliah and ascended the throne of Israel, earning the dubious distinction of becoming the last king of Israel and presiding over the dissolution of the kingdom. In his days, the golden calves no longer stood in Bethel and Dan, not because they had been removed by the kings of Israel but because they had been plundered by Tiglath-Pileser. Hosheia now opened the borders to Judah and allowed his countrymen to go on pilgrimage to the Holy Temple in Jerusalem, but they had drifted too far from God and His Torah to care.[32] The last desperate gasp of hope for a spiritual revival had expired like a whimper on a dying man's lips. The end was only a matter of time.

As the yoke of Assyrian overlordship grew ever heavier, Hosheia ben Eilah turned in despair to decrepit Egypt, the "broken reed"[33] of the Imperial Quadrant, to support his mutiny against Shalmanesser, the king of Assyria. It was worse than useless. Enraged, Shalmanesser invaded Israel and conquered it. In 556 b.c.e., the capital city of Shomron fell after a siege of three years. Then, in a characteristically Assyrian scheme to

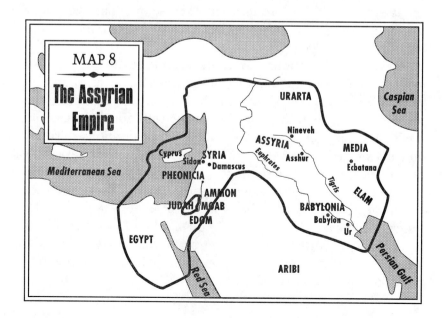

MAP 8

The Assyrian Empire

prevent rebellion, the entire population was deported to Mesopotamia, and other conquered peoples, such as the Cuthites, were brought in to occupy the land. The Kingdom of Israel ceased to exist.

There is no further historical record of the fate of the "Ten Lost Tribes of Israel"; the Talmud debates the question of their eventual return and leaves the matter unresolved.[34] From that point on, the lost tribes entered into the realm of legend. Over the next two millennia, there would be all sorts of legends, rumors and spurious reports of sightings from Ethiopia to Tibet, and future messianic movements would almost invariably claim the support of the armies of the Ten Lost Tribes, whose triumphant return was supposedly imminent.

The departure of the Ten Lost Tribes, however, was anything but triumphant. It was the final turn of ignominy and defeat to a downward spiral that had begun with the partition of the kingdom nearly two hundred and fifty years before. The slide had begun immediately when Yeravam ben Nevat had erected the golden calves as an image for the worship of God, and it continued its inexorable descent as not one of the subsequent kings had both the inclination and the courage to remove them[35]; they could not tolerate the thought that the resumption of pilgrimages to Jerusalem might lead to reunification and the loss of their royal throne. Each of these men had the power to change the course of history, yet each one succumbed to the lust for personal power.

In retrospect, although we cannot condone their actions, we can at least fathom the thinking of the pagans such as Ahab who were fashionably polytheistic in their outlooks. However, the idealistic ones, such as Jehu, present us with an enigma. What could they have been thinking? What rationalizations did they concoct in their own minds for the perpetuation of Yeravam's abominations? Did they perhaps tell themselves that association with Judah was dangerous because of the pagan background of the royal house and that the golden calves were therefore the lesser of two evils? Or did they simply hunker down their heads and refuse to consider such unpleasant thoughts? Yet underneath, they were undoubtedly motivated by the hunger for power and glory during their fleeting sojourn on this earth. The

Talmud teaches that jealousy, desire and the pursuit of honor remove a person from the world.[36] In the case of the kings of Israel, it removed an entire kingdom from the world.

The Kingdom of Judah now stood alone. The indestructible core element of the Jewish people, the steadfast inhabitants of the south and the conscientious dissenters from the north who had found refuge among them, clung to the Holy Temple in Jerusalem, but all was not well in the rest of the kingdom.

For over a century after the execution of the evil queen Asaliah during the reign of Jehu, the Kingdom of Judah had remained free of pagan contamination and enjoyed relative stability and prosperity. Yoash, the grandson of Asaliah who had been secreted in the Temple and crowned at the age of seven, reigned for forty years. He was succeeded by his son Amatziah, who reigned for twenty-nine years, his grandson Uziah, who reigned for thirty-seven years, and his great-grandson Yosam, who reigned for sixteen years. All of these kings were good men, loyal to God and the Torah, but they were unable to break the national habit of sacrificing on private altars.

The stubborn persistence of this unforgivable practice was symptomatic of a deeper malaise that had taken root in Judah. In the days of Rechavam two centuries before, the fire of total devotion to God on a national scale had flickered and died, and the people no longer "sought God" in the truest sense of the word. As generation followed generation, parents could not convey to their children that which they themselves did not have, and thus, the practice of Judaism continued in a dutiful but uninspired and apathetic manner for two hundred years. Therefore, they could not be persuaded to abandon the convenient habits of the private altars by cold logic alone, just as people cannot be dissuaded from engaging in idle gossip by logic alone. Cold logic, no matter how impressive, is only likely to elicit silence and a shrug.

The only way to break this generational cycle of apathy was by lighting a fire under the people, and for two centuries, no one had succeeded in doing so. And although the fire still smoldered amidst the core element of the Jewish people—the Sanhedrin and the Kohanim and the prophets and the Torah scholars and the simple people who loved the Almighty with all their hearts—the conflagration did not spread to the rest of the people.

Why was this so? It is impossible to tell. Perhaps the core element was too small a group to sway the entire population. Perhaps the apathy was so deeply ingrained that only a leader with the authority and charisma of a Joshua or a Samuel or a David could awaken the people from their spiritual torpor. Certainly, the kings that ruled Judah during these times did not fit this mold, and the great prophets who brought them the Word of God were just voices in the wilderness, not acknowledged leaders of the people.

As time went on, the superficiality of the Torah observance in Judah began to erode the very foundations of society. Lacking higher ideals, the people became materialistic and self-indulgent. Avarice, bribery, deceit, corruption and exploitation of the disadvantaged became commonplace, and the prophets cried out in anguish at the degeneration of Jewish society.

Finally, the inevitable happened. In 575 b.c.e., Achaz succeeded his father Yosam to the throne and established the Baal cult throughout Judah.[37] The virulent pagan germ which had infected the Davidic dynasty through its matrimonial alliances with the House of Ahab in the times of Asa and Yehoshafat, and which had lain dormant for over a century, now triggered a new outbreak of the disease. After all, it was but a small step from hollow observance to the actual shedding of the religious husks that had become no more than an outer skin. Judah was vulnerable. Nevertheless, upon reflection, it is difficult to grasp why at this particular juncture the people of Judah should have accepted the pagan initiatives of the new king.

The times were dangerous and convulsive. The rising Assyrian Empire was the most powerful and most ruthless conqueror ever to threaten the region, and although Achaz had declined to join an alliance against Assyria on the advice of the prophet Isaiah, the peril was still great. The neighboring Kingdom of Israel, even while suffering its final death throes under Pekach ben Remaliah and Hosheia ben Eilah, had formed an alliance with Syria and attacked Judah. In the south, Egypt watched the growing Assyrian power with alarm, and it seemed likely that the inevitable battlefield confrontation between the rising and declining powers would draw Judah into the conflict. Times like these call for prudence, temperance and clear vision; good judgment is critical for survival.

Thus, even if the people did not have a profound belief in divine providence and the direct relationship between national calamity and national iniquity, surely they should have discovered in their own history that a descent into paganism had consistently debilitated them and resulted in military reverses. Why take the chance?

From our vantage point twenty-five hundred years in the future, we can only speculate about this question. Perhaps the political situation did not seem as ominous at the time as it seems to our hindsight. Perhaps they thought that by turning to idolatry they would be less "different" from their neighbors and therefore safer. Or perhaps their spiritual apathy and demoralization were so severe that they simply did not give these considerations much thought and simply slid mindlessly into the natural outgrowth of their decadent way of life. It is impossible to know with any degree of certainty.

Yet just at the moment when the night seemed blackest, there was a sudden flash of light which transformed the Kingdom of Judah and lifted it from the nadir of its existence to one the highest points in its history. In 561 b.c.e., Achaz died after sixteen years of unmitigated disaster, and his son Hezekiah ascended to the throne.

Hezekiah, a righteous and charismatic king in the mold of David and Solomon, managed to overcome the spiritual inertia that had gripped Judah for centuries; according to the Talmud, he was so extraordinary that he almost earned for himself the role of the Messiah.[38] Undoubtedly, his stirring portrayals of the misfortune that had befallen the people in the past because of their iniquity had a powerful effect,[39] but his most effective means of changing the mindset of his subjects was by instituting and enforcing a program of intense and universal Torah study. No longer could people limit their study to the laws immediately relevant to the conduct of their lives. No longer was the goal of comprehensive Torah knowledge restricted to Torah scholars and judges. Under this enlightened king, one would have been hard-pressed to find an ignoramus anywhere in the land, and even children had a thorough knowledge of the laws of ritual purity.[40]

As the Jewish people drank deeply of this life-giving elixir which had been in their possession for so many years, a new spirit of vitality and inspiration coursed through their veins. All the idols were destroyed, and for the first time since the days of Solomon, the private altars were also demolished. The Holy Temple was purified, refurbished and rededicated, and the festivals were celebrated with the fierce joy of the new penitent who still shudders with horror at the memory of his recent past.[41] At long last, the people truly "sought God" in their prayer, in their study and in their everyday lives, and the land was illuminated by a great spiritual awakening the likes of which had not taken place for centuries.

Hezekiah now tried to extend this spiritual awakening to the northern kingdom. He sent messengers to Israel, whose borders Hosheia ben Eilah had opened, inviting the people to come to Jerusalem on pilgrimage. Perhaps they could still redeem themselves and avert the terrible fate which hung over their heads. But the messengers were greeted for the most part with scorn and derision. Only a small number of people from Asher, Menasheh and Zevulun swallowed their pride and came to Jerusalem. The rest of the people had drifted too far away. Three years later, their country ceased to exist.

True to the pattern of Jewish history, the spiritual revival sparked by Hezekiah eventually resulted in economic growth and military successes so that Judah became more prosperous and secure than it had been at any time since the days of Solomon. But the shadow of Assyria grew ever darker and longer with the passage of time. The Assyrians had conquered Babylon and all the rest of Mesopotamia, as well as Syria and Israel. The addition of Judah and Egypt was all the Assyrians needed to gain total control of the Quadrant.

In 546 b.c.e., fourteen years into Hezekiah's reign, Sennacherib led an Assyrian army of one hundred and eighty-five thousand men into Judah and laid siege to Jerusalem. The city's fortifications had been reinforced and ample supplies of food and water had been stocked, but the prospect of war between the Assyrian colossus and the shrunken Jewish enclave of Judah struck terror into the hearts of the people. The king, however, encouraged them to take heart in the knowledge that they were far stronger than Assyria because God was on their side. Then the king and Isaiah prayed together for salvation, and during the night, the Assyrian soldiers encamped around Jerusalem mysteriously died. Sennacherib fled to Nineveh where he was assassinated by his sons while sacrificing to his gods.[42]

The story of the miraculous destruction of Sennacherib's camp has been confirmed in recent years by archaeological excavations. An Egyptian imitation, reported by Herodotus,[43] claims that it took place at the border of Egypt where field mice overran the Assyrian camp and ate all the leather straps and weapon handles. Modern historians, perplexed by this amazing occurrence, offer explanations ranging from an outbreak of bubonic plague to a pinpoint barrage of meteorites caused by the entry of Mars into the planetary system.[44] But whatever the actual instrument of destruction, it was clearly a supernatural event, similar to the Jewish victory at Jericho in the times of Joshua. God had allowed the Jewish people to stand back while He Himself fought their battle. The people of the Kingdom of Judah were thus spared the fate of their cousins to the north. The Assyrian menace receded, and the independence of Judah was not threatened again for another century.

Seven hundred years earlier, the Jewish nation had stood at the foot of Mount Sinai and received the Torah from God. Armed with the spiritual weapons of the Torah, they had gone forth to combat the imaginary god race that dominated the ancient world and proclaim the Kingdom of God. It had been a war of ebb and flow, a war of victories and also defeats.

The remaining warriors now gathered in the tiny Kingdom of Judah, the tribes of Judah and Benjamin, the Kohanim and the Levites, the remnants of the other tribes who had fled to the south. Yet surprisingly, the war was not lost, because victory in a spiritual war does not depend on the number of soldiers but on the intensity of commitment. Under Hezekiah, the people had rediscovered intense commitment; they sought God. For all the suffering of the past, the future glowed with promise and hope.

7

Exile and Return

*As you have forsaken Me and served
strange gods in your own land, so shall
you serve strangers in a land which is
not yours.*

(Jeremiah 5:19)

I n 533 b.c.e., after a reign of twenty-five years, Hezekiah was succeeded by his son Menasheh, who was twelve years old when he became king. Menasheh ruled for fifty-five years, the longest reign in Jewish history—and the worst. Menasheh destroyed everything his father Hezekiah had accomplished, and by the time he was through, the Kingdom of Judah had exceeded the basest forms of paganism it had known during the reign of Achaz.

It is difficult to understand why a young prince raised in the royal palace of the saintly Hezekiah should be inclined to such evil. Perhaps some traumatic experience activated the dormant toxins of the blood of Ahab and Jezebel that flowed in his young veins. Perhaps the influence of his mother Hepzebah was in some way responsible.[1] But whatever his motivations may have been, he broke new ground in villainy and depravity.

Far more difficult to understand is how the people of Judah

allowed themselves to be subverted by Menasheh. The light of Torah had shone more brightly during the reign of Hezekiah than at any time since the days of Solomon. How could they have fallen so far in the matter of a few short years?

The answer is to be found in the crucial role of generational conditioning, which we sometimes tend to underestimate. At first glance, it would seem that only people with whom we come into direct contact can influence our attitudes and beliefs. After all, how can we be affected by what our ancestors thought and did in the previous century? But the truth is that the attitudes and beliefs of our distant ancestors have an exceedingly powerful influence on our lives.

The Talmud, with its astonishing wisdom, advises that one refrain from making critical remarks about gentiles in front of the descendants of righteous converts for ten generations.[2] Although these thoroughly Jewish descendants of converts are very far removed from their gentile forbears in time and ideology, there still remains a tenuous connection that is not so easily severed. This residual connection manifests itself in thousands of minuscule subliminal and subconscious nuances that are cumulatively significant. The passage of each generation, however, filters out more and more of these nuances. By the tenth generation, they are all gone, and the connection is severed. Such is the power of generational conditioning.

Conversely, the longer successive generations adhere to a particular ideology or way of life, the more ingrained it becomes. All the fine nuances of thought and life are winnowed through the filters of each passing generation until they become indelibly imprinted on the souls of posterity.

The shaded flavors of a child's upbringing—the attitudes, the inflections, the rhythms, the humor, the habits, the fears and the hopes—all color his being with the deep-hued dyes of background and identity. Newly acquired attitudes and beliefs, however, no matter how strongly held, do not merge into the fibers of the soul. The intellect is more easily transformed than the identity, and only by generational conditioning do the intellect and the identity become one.

The Kingdom of Judah had undergone a tremendous transformation under Hezekiah. The dismal fate of its sister kingdom

to the north and the charismatic leadership of the noble
Hezekiah had combined to diffuse the spirit of the core element to all levels of society. But generational conditioning in
the new mode was lacking. Actually, generational conditioning
worked against the Jewish people, since they had become con-
ditioned for centuries to an apathetic and mechanical observance of the Torah. Thus, although the light of Torah did
indeed burst forth and illuminate Hezekiah's kingdom, it was
only a luminous garment worn on the exterior of the soul. It
would take generations of continuity for that garment to fuse
with the soul that it clothed, but those generations never came
to pass. Menashe would not let it happen.

The Talmud tells us that three kings have no share in the
afterlife—Yeravam, Ahab and Menasheh.[3] Yeravam started the
nation on its downward spiral by erecting the golden calves as
images of worship, thus undermining the Jewish concept of
divinity and ultimately causing the downfall of both kingdoms.
Ahab took advantage of the debilitated spiritual state of the
Jewish people and introduced outright idol worship to the
Kingdom of Israel, but with customary pagan tolerance, he did
not outlaw the study or observance of the Torah. Menasheh,
however, was an altogether different story. After a quarter century of Hezekiah's enlightened rule, the people were intellectually opposed to the idea of a return to paganism, and Menasheh
could therefore not afford to be tolerant and patient. Instead,
resorting to cunning and brute force, he mounted a frontal
assault on the Torah in order to accomplish his sinister goals.

Menasheh's gambit was the reintroduction of the forbidden
practice of sacrificing to God on private altars.[4] Menasheh probably claimed this would be a step forward in piety and observance, and presumably, he drew on his considerable erudition[5]
to rationalize this violation of the Torah. The core element of
the Jewish people was, of course, not fooled by this ploy, but the
weaker elements were deceived. The volatile segment of the
population that swung back and forth like a pendulum between
observance and paganism did not look to the Sanhedrin, the
Kohanim and the Torah scholars for leadership and guidance.
Traditionally, they were inclined to follow the lead of their
kings. Hezekiah had been successful in leading them in one

direction. Menasheh, with cleverness and subtlety, was now steering them in the opposite direction.

Once Menasheh succeeded in breaching the wall of universal Torah observance, the old habits and rhythms not yet filtered out by generational conditioning began to reappear. Before long, Menasheh felt confident enough to shed his pretense of piety. He declared his fervent allegiance to the god race and built places of worship in their honor.

Menasheh was right in his assessment of the people. The fickle elements allowed themselves to be drawn into the pagan frenzy. But there was also a great deal of outrage and opposition, because the Torah had sunk deep roots during the days of Hezekiah. Menasheh responded by declaring war on God, so to speak. He banned the Torah and slaughtered its most ardent adherents so that "Jerusalem was filled from end to end with innocent blood"[6]; among his victims was the prophet Isaiah,[7] who was himself a member of the royal family.[8] Then, in a burst of flagrant blasphemy, Menasheh took a pagan altar built by his grandfather Achaz and brought it into the Sanctuary of the Holy Temple. For all his iniquity, Achaz would never have dared do it, but Menasheh had much broader support.[9]

Menasheh continued his mutiny against God and his attack on the Torah for twenty-two years,[10] and by his combination of subterfuge and brutality, he devastated Judah as never before. The core element went into virtual hiding in order to continue observing the Torah, and the rest of the people flocked to the pagan temples.

In the twenty-third year of his reign, Menasheh was captured during an Assyrian incursion and taken in chains to a prison in Babylon. In the dark dungeon, Menasheh saw the light that had eluded him in the royal palace, and he prayed to the God of his fathers for deliverance. His prayers were answered, and he was released and restored to his throne. But the die was cast. For the remaining thirty-three years of his reign, he campaigned vigorously against the Baal cult he himself had introduced to Judah, but to no avail. The people had been subverted, and Menasheh lacked the moral authority to rectify completely the damage he had done.[11]

The Kingdom of Judah had hit rock bottom. It had become

morally corrupt, drained of its grace and holiness, a hotbed of
pagan culture in which the Torah was actively persecuted. The
last reprieve had been exhausted, and the Divine Presence
withdrew from its Abode in Jerusalem.[12] It was now only a matter
of time before the kingdom itself would crumble and collapse.
The experiment of the Kings had ended in abject failure. The
delicate instrument of the spiritual monarchy of Judah had
been introduced prematurely, and it was now encrusted with
blood and moral rot. The villainous Menasheh had made a
travesty of the aspirations of the Jewish people and the divine
mission of the Davidic dynasty, and in the process, he had
caused the destruction of the Jewish kingdom and all the tribu-
lations of exile that arose from it.

In 478 b.c.e., Menasheh was succeeded by his son Amon, a
fanatical pagan who tried to bring back the Baal cult as in the
early days of his father's reign. He attacked the Jewish religion
with peculiar vindictiveness, ordering the consignment of Torah scrolls to the flames and the cessation of the Temple service.
Faithful Jews were now forced to practice their religion in secret
in their own homeland. In the Temple, a thunderous silence
replaced the exuberant clamor of the holy service, and the altar
languished under a shroud of spider webs.[13] It seemed that
nothing less than the complete obliteration of Judaism would
satisfy Amon.

In 476 b.c.e., two years after he ascended the throne, Amon
was assassinated in the palace by the royal guard. An enraged
mob stormed the palace and killed all the rebels. Then they
placed Amon's eight-year-old son Yoshiahu on the throne without the customary anointing of the king by a prophet of God.
The rabble of the streets had usurped the coronation process.
The kingdom was clearly disintegrating.

Nevertheless, Yoshiahu was a gallant captain of the sinking
ship of state. Although raised in a pagan environment, he was
already gravitating to the pure faith of his ancestors at the age of
sixteen. In 464 b.c.e, at the age of twenty, he courageously
undertook to repair the damage inflicted on the kingdom by his
father and grandfather for six decades. He began the laborious
process of purging Judah of pagan contamination and refur-
bishing the Holy Temple. It promised to be a difficult task, for it

involved not only removing the physical trappings but also re-conditioning the hearts and minds of the people.

In 458 b.c.e., a startling discovery shocked the nation. The original Torah scroll written by Moses nearly one thousand years before was found in the Sanctuary of the Temple, where it had been secreted during the times of persecution.[14] It was open to the *Tochachah*, the Reproof Section of *Deuteronomy*, specifically to the verses, "God shall deport you and the king you appoint for yourselves to a nation unknown to you or your fathers, and you will be subservient to alien gods of wood and stone. And you will be desolate, ridiculed and mocked by all the peoples wherever God will deliver you."[15]

This unmistakable portent triggered intense consternation among the king and his advisors. Moreover, having been installed by the mob without prophetic sanction, Yoshiahu was certain that he was "the king you appoint for yourselves."[16] He wept and rent his garments, and he sent the High Priest to consult the prophets.

Five years earlier, the great Jeremiah had begun to prophesy in the Kingdom of Judah. At the time of this crisis, however, he was absent from Jerusalem, and instead, the High Priest consulted the prophetess Chuldah, who lived in Jerusalem.[17] The prophetess confirmed the approaching calamity, but she reassured the king that because of his submission to God the destruction would not occur during his lifetime.

Chuldah's message sparked the last great spiritual revival in the Kingdom of Judah. The king convened an assembly of the people in the Holy Temple, and he informed them of what had transpired. Then he proclaimed a covenant to reaffirm the Jewish commitment to God and His Torah, and the people solemnly voiced their acceptance.

From that point on, the purge was no longer slow and laborious. Indeed, it became a veritable frenzy that surpassed any of the earlier purges. In a few short months, every last vestige of idolatrous worship and private altars was destroyed. All animals, utensils and artifacts with any idolatrous connection whatsoever were incinerated in huge pyres in the valley outside Jerusalem, and their ashes were scattered on the graves of idol worshippers. The purge then spread into the virtually vacant lands of the former Kingdom of Israel. The altars of Yeravam in Bethel and Dan were finally torn down, torched and ground to dust along with any other trace of idolatry that remained in the forlorn countryside.

At long last, there were no visible signs of the pagan penetration of Jewish society, but the invisible stains were too deep to be so quickly expunged. An uneasy quiet descended on the land for the next thirteen years, but it was like living in the shadow of a smoking volcano. Internally, a revitalized Jewish society did not materialize; the people still harbored pagan sentiments, which they had renounced only out of abject fear, and many still practiced the pagan rites in secret.[18] Externally, tensions between the declining Assyrian colossus in the north and the obdurate Egyptian kingdom in the south were reaching a fever pitch, and the tiny Kingdom of Judah lay directly in the path of confrontation. The ground beneath the doomed Jewish kingdom shook and trembled, riven by the forces of inexorable fate.

In 445 b.c.e., an Egyptian army under Pharaoh Necho crossed the border of the Kingdom of Judah and headed north to drive Assyrian invaders from the Aramean city of Carcemish on the Euphrates River. Yoshiahu denied the Egyptians the use of his country as a war corridor, and he mustered an army to block their passage in the valley of Meggido. In the ensuing battle, Yoshiahu was killed by Egyptian archers, and the Jewish forces withdrew. The Egyptians went on to defeat the Assyrians at the First Battle of Carcemish, gaining temporary suzerainty over the entire region south of Syria in the vacuum created by the collapsing Assyrian Empire.

After the death of Yoshiahu, mob rule once again determined the succession to the crown. Without prophetic sanction, the mob passed over Yoshiahu's oldest son Eliyakim and chose his younger brother Yehoachaz as the new king. Yehoachaz turned out to be a throwback to Menashe and Amon, which was undoubtedly why the mob had wanted him in the first place. But they need not have worried, for events would show that Eliyakim was no better than his younger brother.

Three months later, Pharaoh Necho replaced the vengeful Yehoachaz, who was harassing Egypt,[19] with the elder Eliyakim, who accepted Egyptian overlordship; Necho also changed

Eliyakim's name to Yehoakim to underscore his control of the Jewish king.[20] Necho had chosen well. Yehoakim proved to be an obsequious Egyptian puppet, ever eager to please his avaricious master. As depraved as his deposed brother, Yehoakim made a mockery of his illustrious father's desperate efforts to save the kingdom. Paganism once again spread among the common people like a stubborn cancer that refused to respond to treatment, and Jewish society was once again devastated by the dissolution of religious life and the breakdown of morality and simple decency.

Nevertheless, despite the dire prophecies and the fall from grace, the Jewish people still retained freedom of choice; to an extent, their fate was in their own hands. Even in the final doomed days of Judah, the gates of repentance were clearly not sealed shut. "Thus said the God of Hosts . . ." Jeremiah prophesied during Yehoakim's reign. "For if you truly mend your ways and deeds, if you truly execute justice between one man and another, you will not exploit the stranger, orphan or widow, nor will you spill innocent blood in this place, nor will you follow alien gods to your own detriment. Only then will I allow you to dwell in this place, in the land I gave your forefathers always and forever."[21] But Jeremiah's words fell on deaf ears, and the death watch of the kingdom continued.

Meanwhile, important changes were taking place in Mesopotamia. The collapse of the Assyrian Empire resulted in a shift of power to the ancient city of Babylon, an immense metropolis covering many square miles and having millions of inhabitants. Although Nineveh had been the capital of the Assyrian Empire, Babylon had been its most important city; Babylon had played New York to Nineveh's Washington. Practically an entire nation unto itself, Babylon was the economic, religious and cultural capital of Mesopotamia, and now it also became the political capital.

Four years into Yehoakim's reign, in 441 b.c.e., a Babylonian army under Nebuchadnezzar crushed the Egyptian forces at the Second Battle of Carcemish and drove the Egyptians back behind their own borders.[22] The Kingdom of Judah now passed back into the Mesopotamian sphere of influence, and Yehoakim became a Babylonian vassal. In 438 b.c.e., expecting a new resurgence in Egyptian power, Yehoakim rebelled and refused to pay tribute to his Babylonian masters. For four years, he lived on borrowed time as Nebuchadnezzar secured the eastern borders of his empire, but stripped of Babylonian protection, the Kingdom of Judah now fell victim to repeated raids by Chaldean, Aramean, Moabite and Ammonite marauders.

In 434 b.c.e., Nebuchadnezzar finally turned his attentions to the mettlesome little Jewish kingdom. Nebuchadnezzar overran the country, raided the Holy Temple, arrested Yehoakim and took him in chains to Babylon, where he died in disgrace.

Yehoakim was succeeded by his eighteen-year-old son Yehoachin, who was cut from the same cloth as his father and uncle, both in his pagan sympathies and in his unwillingness to submit to Babylonian domination. He bolstered the fortifications of Jerusalem,[23] and waited hopefully for Egyptian support. It was not forthcoming.

Three short months after Yehoachin became king, Nebuchadnezzar laid siege to Jerusalem. Yehoachin gave himself up to Nebuchadnezzar, along with the royal family and ministers, as a sign of submission, but it was not enough for Nebuchadnezzar. He took ten thousand additional captives, as well as some more booty from the Holy Temple, and returned to Babylon, where Yehoachin was imprisoned.

Before he left, Nebuchadnezzar took Mattaniah, Yehoachin's twenty-one-year-old uncle, changed his name to Tzidkiahu and placed him on the vacated throne. Tzidkiahu thus became the third son of Yoshiahu and the twenty-second member of the House of David to become king of Judah. He also had the dubious distinction of being its last king. For all its shortcomings, this illustrious dynasty had provided the Kingdom of Judah with the stability of uninterrupted patrilineal succession for four and a half centuries. The kingdom and its royal house had become indivisible, and together, they would face their tragic fate.

A true son of his father, Tzidkiahu was a faithful servant of God and a staunch follower of the Torah, but he found himself in an untenable situation. The ten thousand captives that Nebuchadnezzar had carried off to Babylon included the best and the finest in the land, the great Torah scholars, the leaders, the judges, the learned priests, virtually the entire core element of the Jewish people that had clung tenaciously to the sacred Torah regardless of the sentiments of the man who sat on the throne. Nebuchadnezzar had skimmed off the cream of the Jewish people and taken it for himself, leaving only the human sediment that had carried the pagan infection for generations. The faint light of Torah which had still shone during the reign of Yehoachin was now extinguished, and despite Jeremiah's impassioned exhortations, the last pitiful remnants of the kingdom lapsed into total degeneration.

Disheartened, Tzidkiahu resigned himself to the political administration of his kingdom. He did not even attempt to exert a positive spiritual influence on his hapless subjects, and the prophet Jeremiah admonished him for this unforgivable omission in *The Book of Kings*.[24] In spite of their fallen state, these people were still Jews, and their anointed king had no right to despair of them and turn inward in the waning days of the kingdom.

In one aspect, however, Tzidkiahu did share the sentiments of the previous three kings. He chafed under the yoke of Babylonian domination, and against the advice of Jeremiah, he tried to cast it off.[25]

In 425 b.c.e., on the tenth day of the month of Teves, Nebuchadnezzar invaded Judah with a vast army and laid siege to Jerusalem for the last time. Massive siege machines and structures were erected around the embattled city, and the long wait began. The siege lasted for two years, and towards the end, the privations of the people barricaded within the walls of Jerusalem were fearsome. The Jewish kingdom was suffering its final death throes. Spiritually moribund, it was about to perish physically as well.

In 423 b.c.e., on the ninth day of the month of Tammuz, the walls of Jerusalem were breached, and the long-frustrated Babylonian hordes burst into the city. A scene of unimaginable carnage followed, with the bleeding bodies of the slaughtered falling near the emaciated bodies of their brothers and neighbors who had expired from hunger and thirst. Those fortunate few who managed to flee the stricken city scattered to the winds and sought refuge in the neighboring lands; some eventually reached the distant shores of France and Spain.[26]

Tzidkiahu tried to escape through a long subterranean passage which led to Jericho, but he was captured. Nebuchadnezzar made Tzidkiahu watch as all his sons were butchered, then the vindictive Babylonian king put out Tzidkiahu's eyes and sent him off in chains to Babylon, where he died in captivity.[27]

Even as Tzidkiahu was being brought before Nebuchadnezzar, the Temple Mount still held out, but on the seventeenth day of Tammuz, the pressure of the fighting brought a halt to the daily sacrifices.[28] On the seventh day of the month of Av, the invaders penetrated the walls of the Holy Temple and massacred its defenders. They vandalized, ransacked and pillaged the Holy Temple for two days, stripping it bare of all portable valuables, and on the ninth day of the month, they set it ablaze.[29]

As the writhing flames licked at the incarnadine sky, a pall of dense smoke spread over the beautiful Jerusalem hills. The timbers and the fabrics and the finery that had adorned the glorious Abode of the Divine Presence for four hundred and ten years exploded into fiery embers that streaked the dark heavens of the incredulous night. Ashes borne aloft by the heat-driven winds rained down on the remains of the fallen kingdom

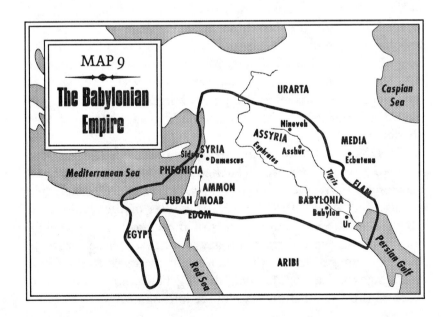

MAP 9

The Babylonian Empire

and mixed with the blood on its cobblestones and the tears of the captives being led into exile in Babylon. The fires raged through the night and long into the following day, and when they finally subsided, the Jewish homeland which had stood for nearly a thousand years was a smoldering ruin.

Yet even at this point of deepest tragedy, with a millennium of hopes and aspirations reduced to ashes, with the abject failure of the divine Jewish mission to lead humanity to its ultimate destiny, with the kingdom destroyed and its people in captivity, a ray of hope still shone. Before departing for Babylon, Nebuchadnezzar allowed some of the most destitute Jewish survivors to stay on the land, and he appointed Gedaliah ben Achikam to serve as governor of the newly constituted Babylonian colony.

Gedaliah, a noble and devout man of distinguished lineage, encouraged the stunned survivors to resume their normal lives. He reassured them that they need not fear the occupation forces as long as they were loyal to the Babylonian king. Slowly, bedraggled officers and soldiers of the scattered Jewish military forces and a number of returning civilian refugees began to coalesce around Gedaliah's fledgling government at Mitzpah outside Jerusalem. The process of picking up the pieces began.

It was as if, after having exhausted all their last chances, the Jewish people were being given yet another last chance from God's seemingly inexhaustible supply of reprieves. Astonishingly, there still remained a tenuous ligament of attachment between the Jewish people and their ancestral homeland; the exile was still not absolute, and there was still hope. Perhaps this tiny nucleus, stripped of glory and bombast, would find its way back to the ancient Jewish ideals. Perhaps these poverty-stricken derelicts of society would take possession of the vacated fields and vineyards and use the bounty of the land to support true Torah life. Perhaps this humble little seed would sink its slender tendrils into the hallowed soil and bring forth verdant new shoots. But it was not to be.

Among the returnees was an ambitious member of the royal family named Yishmael ben Nessaniah. Upon the instigation of Baalis, the Ammonite king, Yishmael and his followers assassinated Gedaliah and murdered the entire Babylonian garrison.

In the ensuing battle between Yishmael's group and Gedaliah's supporters led by Yochanan ben Koreiach, Yishmael fled to Ammon with only a handful of men. But the damage was done. Fearful of Babylonian retaliation for the massacre of the garrison and disregarding the dire warnings of the prophet Jeremiah, Yochanan led all the remaining Jews to the illusory safety of Egypt, which would fall to the Babylonian Empire eight years later. Only a few short months had elapsed from the destruction of the Temple to the collapse of Gedaliah's administration and the total downfall of Judah.

The exile was complete. The land, empty of its Jewish inhabitants, lay submerged under a blanket of memories without rememberers. The air quivered with the fading sounds of the past. And then there was silence.

In the Jewish localities of Babylon, however, there was anything but silence. Unlike the Assyrians, the Babylonians were astute victors, and the ten thousand captives carried off from Judah eleven years before the destruction of Jerusalem had been treated well. The Babylonians recognized the nobility of the Jewish core element that had maintained its high moral standards in the face of adversity, and they sought to integrate this elite group into the multiethnic tapestry of the Empire. Protected by royal sanction, the Jewish exiles began to lay the foundations of the great Babylonian Jewish community that would endure for a thousand years.

The immediate concern of this first group of exiles was the preservation of the Torah, especially the Oral Law without which the Torah cannot be understood. From the beginning, the Oral Law had been passed down by a system of transmission supervised by the leading Torah sage of each generation. After Joshua, this task had been shouldered by the Judges, the Torah sages who were also the unofficial political leaders. With the rise of the monarchy, the stewardship of the Oral Law had been assumed by the unbroken succession of Prophets, which ran parallel to the royal succession. But now the kingdom was on the verge of collapse, and the dispersion had already begun. Jeremiah had prophesied that the exile would end after seventy years,[30] but what form would the restoration assume? Would there always be prophets to teach the people?[31] And if not, how would the special bond between the Jewish people and God and His Torah be sustained?

Paradoxically, exile and captivity had brought the core element of the Jewish people more freedom than it had enjoyed in a century. In Babylon, there were no corrupt monarchs and pagan enthusiasts to battle for the Jewish soul. Confined to this distant land but breathing the heady air of spiritual freedom, these elite exiles, among whom there were a thousand sages, understood that the future of the Jewish people rested on their shoulders.[32] They knew that it was their mission to form the nucleus of a rejuvenated Jewish nation, and they poured all their energies into creating a solid bedrock of Torah for the future. They established numerous *yeshivos* in all the cities and towns where they settled,[33] and the intense study of the Torah flourished.

The Jewish exiles also prospered economically and politically. They felt comfortable in the bounteous land which had been the birthplace of their ancestor Abraham and whose people spoke Aramaic, a kindred language to their own Hebrew.[34] They built houses and raised families, planted gardens and vineyards and entered the government service. Young Jewish prodigies were taken into the royal palace and groomed for high office; most prominent among these apprentices was Daniel, who rose to ministerial level.

Within a decade, the first exiles were firmly established on Babylonian soil, forming a community that was extraordinarily powerful by any measure. Relatively few in number, they were cohesive, learned, dynamic, wealthy and influential. And now, when the stunned survivors of the destruction of Jerusalem began to stream into Babylon in 423 b.c.e., they found a strong Jewish community awaiting them with open arms and open hearts. Four years later, further Babylonian conquests of Phoenicia, Ammon and Moab, where many Jews had sought refuge, produced a new wave of exiles to Babylon.[35] Eight years later, in 415 b.c.e., the conquest of Egypt and its Jewish refugee settlements added the last wave of exiles to the burgeoning Jewish community of Babylon; among them were the aged Jeremiah and his foremost disciple Baruch ben Neriah.[36]

The disease of paganism had finally been purged from the

Jewish people. The horrors of the siege and fall of Jerusalem had brought the people to their senses, and even if some still harbored secret pagan sympathies, the Jewish community of Babylon was too tightly constructed along strict Torah lines to be affected by them; the new waves of exiles, although far more numerous, were absorbed on the terms of the original exiles. The Jewish settlements spread, prospered and flourished in a burst of growth that caught the attention of their Babylonian hosts, but the Jewish people resisted assimilation. Bolstered by the hopeful prophesies of Ezekiel, they remained insular and steadfastly loyal to the Torah.

In 397 b.c.e., Eveel Merudach succeeded his father Nebuchadnezzar to the Babylonian throne. One of his first acts as king was to release the Jewish king Yehoachin from prison, where he had moldered for thirty-seven years. The prophet Jeremiah saw fit to conclude *The Book of Kings* with a lengthy account of Yehoachin's reinstatement as king of the Jews and his receiving first honors among the other vassal kings of the Babylonian Empire. Clearly, Jeremiah saw this as a sign of divine grace amidst the exile. The Jewish nation had been reborn in exile, just as it had been born in the Egyptian exile a thousand years before. The Jewish nation was once again afire with the spirit of the Torah, secure, prosperous and respected, a self-governing kingdom in microcosm transplanted from its homeland into Babylonian exile.

But it was exile nonetheless. And as the wounds healed and the normal rhythms of life returned, the people sat by the rivers of Babylon and wept for the loss of their sacred homeland, for the blood that was shed and for glorious Jerusalem that was no more. But most of all, they wept for their estrangement from the Divine Presence that had resided in the Holy Temple. "For this, our hearts were sorrowful," they lamented. "For these, our eyesight blurred. For Mount Zion that lay in ruins, foxes scampered upon it. You, O God, shall reign eternal, Your throne will last for all generations. Why do You forget us forever? Why do you abandon us for the longest time? Bring us back to You, O God, and we will return. Renew our days as of old."[37] Security and hope could ease the pain but not remove it completely.

As we look back at the first fifty years of the exile in Babylon, we are struck by the similarities to the early years of some of the subsequent Jewish diaspora communities. The Jews had been brought to Babylon for the benefit of the host country, and through talent, industry and solidarity, they rapidly achieved disproportionate influence and wealth. This pattern of Jewish exile would be repeated again and again.

In later years, we see the Jews invited to Poland in the twelfth century to serve as a national middle class, and we see King Frederick invite Jews to Berlin in the sixteenth century to help him build an empire; in each case, the Jews rapidly surpassed the indigenous population. In the seventeenth century, we see mercantile competition with Holland cause Oliver Cromwell to readmit Jews to Great Britain, and in the nineteenth century, we see Jews welcomed to the shores of America, along with all other immigrants; in each case, the Jews rose quickly to the top.

As we continue to trace the pattern of the Babylonian experience, the uncanny foreshadowing of the future persists, and developments take an ominous turn.

For over a century, the vassal kingdoms of Media and Persia in northern Mesopotamia had consolidated their power under the umbrella of imperial Assyria and then Babylon. The two kingdoms were related by intermarriage between the royal houses and a confluence of interests. For generations, they had sought to expand their sphere of influence northward into the Greek states of Asia Minor and beyond to Scythia, the site of present-day Russia. A number of disastrous wars with the tenacious Greeks, however, convinced them of the ultimate futility of such an endeavor and diverted their expansionist ambitions southward towards the imperial centers of Mesopotamia itself.

In 372 b.c.e., Darius, the king of Media, formed an alliance with his son-in-law Cyrus, the king of Persia, the result of which was a virtual union between the two kingdoms. Together, the Persian and Median forces conquered Babylon and killed Balshazzar, the son and successor of Eveel Merudach. Darius, known to history as Darius the Mede, became the first king of the new empire, and the imperial capital was established in the Median capital of Ecbatana. Under Darius, the Jews continued to prosper, and the talented Daniel became the vizier of the empire. In 371 b.c.e., Darius was killed on the battlefield. He was succeeded by his Persian son-in-law Cyrus, who moved the imperial capital to Shushan (Susa) in Persia.

One of Cyrus's first acts as emperor was to authorize the Jews to return to Jerusalem and rebuild the Holy Temple. The proclamation sparked great rejoicing among the Jews, because it signalled the end of their captivity. Most Babylonians Jews, however, chose not to avail themselves of their newfound freedom. After a half century of adjustment, they had settled into a comfortable existence, both spiritually and financially, and they were not prepared to uproot their families and face the hardships and vicissitudes of reclaiming the desolate ancestral lands. Instead, they offered financial support to the returnees and bided their time. A significant number of Jews, however, did relocate to Shushan when the seat of the imperial government shifted to the Persian capital.

In the same year of Cyrus's proclamation, some forty thousand Jews set out from Babylon to Jerusalem under the leadership of Zerubavel ben Shealtiel, a descendant of the Davidic dynasty. They set up camp among the overgrown rubble of the

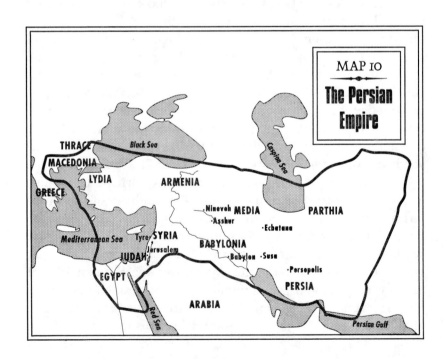

MAP 10

The Persian Empire

city under the suspicious scrutiny of the tribes who occupied the land, and they began to build the Second Temple. Not unexpectedly, problems immediately developed.

The Samaritans, natives of Cutha who had been resettled in Shomron by the Assyrians two centuries before, offered to assist the construction. Suspecting that they intended sabotage, Zerubavel politely declined their offer. The Samaritans immediately revealed their true colors and began harassing and terrorizing the settlers in order to disrupt the progress of the work. In 370 b.c.e., the Samaritans wrote to Cyrus accusing the Jews of seditious intent, and Cyrus withdrew his authorization. The work ground to a halt, and the embattled Jewish community stagnated among the stark reminders of the ruined past and the interrupted present.

In 369 b.c.e., Achashverosh[38] succeeded Cyrus to the Persian throne. Unlike his predecessors, he was hostile to the Jews. He removed Daniel from power and confirmed the suspension of the construction of the Holy Temple. Nevertheless, the wealth and influence of the Jews within the borders of the empire continued to grow. Then, in 357 b.c.e., an incident took place in Shushan that chillingly foreshadowed an all too common experience of the eventual Jewish diaspora.

As chronicled by the sage Mordechai in *The Book of Esther*, a high Persian courtier of Amalekite lineage named Haman convinced Achashverosh to sanction the extermination and pillage of his Jewish subjects. The queen at the time was Mordechai's niece Esther; she had been coerced into marrying the king but had never revealed her Jewish identity. With great courage, and the support of her people who fasted and prayed, the queen foiled Haman's plans and brought about his downfall.

The Jewish people realized that their deliverance had been miraculous, and in commemoration, Mordechai established the annual festival of *Purim*, during which *The Book of Esther* is read in its entirety. But in the entire book, there is no mention of God, who had wrought these miracles, because the Hand of God had been concealed. There were no supernatural occurrences; the sea did not split, there were no pillars of fire, nor did the sun stand still in the sky. There was only providence manipulating ordinary events. And in the future, when the Jewish people would survive calamity after calamity without the force of arms but through providence alone, the story of Esther would glow as a beacon of hope and inspiration in the darkest of times.

In 355 b.c.e., Achashverosh was succeeded by his son Darius II. More favorably inclined toward the Jews, Darius rescinded the suspension orders of Cyrus and Achashverosh, and in 353 b.c.e., the construction of the Holy Temple resumed—exactly seventy years after the destruction, as prophesied by Jeremiah. Four years later, it was completed.

The restoration of a Jewish national entity in the ancestral homeland had begun, but the construction of the Temple was only a small beginning. Unlike the First Temple which had been built as the crowning glory of Solomon's mature and successful kingdom, the Second Temple was built while the majority of Jews remained in Mesopotamia; it was a cornerstone rather than a crown. For the most part, the work of molding the new society still lay ahead. The great leap forward came in 348 b.c.e., a year after the Second Temple was completed.

During the Babylonian captivity, the Jews had formed a ruling council of one hundred and twenty sages known to history as the Anshei Knesses Hagedolah, the Men of the Great Assembly. Most of the members of this august body were prophets, and all were outstanding teachers of the Torah. They included venerable sages, such as Baruch ben Neriah, Mordechai, Daniel, Chananiah, Mishael, Azariah, Ezekiel, Zerubavel and Ezra, who still remembered the First Temple, as well as those born in exile, such as Nechemiah and Simon the Just. Because of his advanced age, Baruch ben Neriah, the foremost disciple of Jeremiah, had been unable to travel to Jerusalem, and the sages remained at his side.[39] But in 348 b.c.e., he passed away, and the sages, with the brilliant and dynamic Ezra at their head, left for Jerusalem with the full blessings of Darius, who extended them royal protection and exempted them from all taxes and levies.[40]

When the Anshei Knesses Hagedolah arrived in Jerusalem, their immediate concern was the amelioration of the existing community. For nearly two decades, the infant community of Jerusalem had been in virtually suspended animation because of the interruption of the Temple construction. They had lived with constant peril and uncertainty, without the energizing focus of a perceptible goal and without the strong Torah underpinnings enjoyed by Babylonian Jews. The community had begun to erode, and some people actually intermarried with the local populace. Although there were only several dozen cases of intermarriage, it was still thoroughly intolerable. Moreover, under the present circumstances, it threatened to sabotage from the start any prospects there might be for a national revitalization.

With their enormous prestige, the Anshei Knesses Hagedolah quickly effected the separation of the intermarried couples and organized a public and universal pledge of fealty to God and His Torah by the entire community. They also solidified the Torah infrastructure of the budding community and tended to its various organizational needs. Then they turned to the critical concern of securing the future.

The Anshei Knesses Hagedolah were faced with entirely new circumstances that presented more unknowns than precedents. Politically, the return to Jerusalem could not be viewed as a resumption of a briefly interrupted historical progression. The Jewish people had not been allowed to reconstitute their kingdom and recover their political independence. They had merely been allowed to resettle as Persian subjects in their ancestral lands which had become a Persian colony. Moreover, most of the people had remained in Babylon and the other scattered communities of the exile. Clearly, the future spiritual guidance of the Jewish people would not derive from political institutions such as the Davidic dynasty.

Furthermore, drastic changes in the geopolitical situation were hastening the end of the age of prophecy, another pillar of pre-exilic Jewish society. Prophecy required a certain serenity of mind and spirit as a prerequisite for the temporary transformation of the human mind into a transcendent channel for divine communication.[41] In former times, despite the occasional outbreaks of war, society had been stable enough to allow people to attain such a state of mind with fair regularity. But the increased frequency, ferocity and sophistication of war throughout the Imperial Quadrant had destabilized society so that a person never knew what tomorrow would bring. Prophecy could not be expected to survive in such a high-anxiety environment.[42]

It seemed obvious to the Anshei Knesses Hagedolah that in order for the Torah to survive on the tempestuous seas of history it would have to be equipped with doctrinal armor that would make it virtually self-propelled. When leadership faltered and prophecy faded, the Torah itself would carry its bearers forward to their rendezvous with destiny. The Torah had commanded the Jewish people not to "deviate to the right or the left from the directives of the sages,"[43] thus conferring Scriptural authority on Rabbinic ordinances designed to safeguard but not alter the Torah.[44] This legislative power had been exercised from time to time to a limited extent,[45] but now it would have to be brought to bear with great urgency and broad scope. The Anshei Knesses Hagedolah prepared to "build a fence around the Torah,"[46] a protective wall to withstand any violent assault that might emanate from the arsenal of history. There was no time to waste.

One can well imagine the weight of the burden borne by these venerable prophets and sages. These men, most of them well into their eighties and nineties, stood together at the crossroads of destiny, a living bridge between an old world that had perished and a nascent world whose character was yet unknown; they knew that the institutions, regulations and guidelines they would devise at this critical juncture would determine the future of their people. Amazingly, these elderly sages discovered within themselves unexpected founts of youthful vigor, and they plunged into the mammoth task of building the Torah edifice that has survived intact to this very day.

With the imminent passing of the age of prophecy, their first attentions were focused on sealing the Scriptures against any further inclusions. They carefully reviewed all the recorded prophecies and chronicles, and they decided which would be considered canonical; only these books would have the force of Torah revelation to be accepted without question. Thus, the books of *Ezra, Nehemiah, Chaggai, Zechariah* and *Malachi*, written by members of the Anshei Knesses Hagedolah with regards to their own times, completed the Bible and brought the Biblical period to a close. At that point, the Anshei Knesses Hagedolah officially declared the Scriptures complete and forever sealed. This barrier would prove immensely significant five hundred years later when the Christians would attempt to force their Gospels into the Jewish Biblical canon.

The Anshei Knesses Hagedolah then turned to the prayers and blessings.[47] Although thrice daily prayers and the blessings had been a central tenet of Judaism from patriarchal times, there had never been an established liturgical text. During Biblical times, which had been characterized by stellar highs and abysmal lows, the core element "sought God" without the confining strictures of liturgical formulae. They prayed according to an accepted pattern but with an adventurous expansion of the soul in ecstatic communion with God. In spontaneous language that mirrored their emotions, they proclaimed their gratitude to God for His bounty and beseeched His favor for all their spiritual and material needs. But in the diminished state of the post-Biblical period, people could not be expected to achieve ecstasy thrice daily. Instead of their emotions giving rise to their prayers, the prayers were needed to stimulate their emotions.

The extraordinary success of the Anshei Knesses Hagedolah in the formulation of the blessings and prayers is manifest to every Jew who prays daily. One would think that a liturgical formula repeated so often would soon become stale and tedious, but the exact opposite is true. The formal Jewish liturgy is among the most brilliant literary achievements ever. Eternally fresh and endlessly inspiring, it weaves the most moving Biblical passages into the elegant and eloquent patterns of the liturgy and wraps the whole composition around a complex intellectual framework; each segment fulfills a specific role and function so that the whole pulsates with a powerful rhythm that adapts constantly to the calendar, communal events and the needs of the individual.

The Talmud describes many other "fences" and regulations attributed to Ezra and the Anshei Knesses Hagedolah with regards to Torah study, religious observance and community affairs. But perhaps most important of all was their initiation of a program upon which the very survival of the Oral Law would depend.

For a thousand years, the Oral Law, like all vast fields of knowledge, had been taught without a formal lexicon of instruction. For instance, a teacher of medicine or mathematics tries to impart his knowledge in his own words in the manner he deems best. He rarely has his students memorize specifically worded phrases. Similarly, teachers of the Oral Law following accepted patterns of instruction were free to employ their tutorial talents as they saw fit and approach their subjects from any angle they chose. In cases of dispute, however, the teachers of the Oral Law were in a weaker position. A teacher of medicine or mathematics could always refer back to his textbooks, but there were no textbooks for the Oral Law.[48] Instead, the prophets served as the final arbiters of all legal questions.[49] But with the age of prophecy coming to an end, other devices, short of permitting a written record, were needed for the preservation of the integrity of the Oral Law.

Once again, the Anshei Knesses Hagedolah turned to the device of formulation which had served them so well in the reinforcement of prayer. They composed a condensed lexicon that encapsulated the fundamental issues of the entire spectrum of the Oral Law. The formalized lexicon, which was to be memorized by all students, would provide a universally accepted mnemonic for the Oral Law and curtail the incidence of disagreements. It was a compromise between actual inscription and the absolute informality of the Biblical period, preserving the knowledge of the Oral Law while protecting its exclusivity to the Jewish people. With decreasing effectiveness, this lexicon worked as a spoken text for five hundred years when, with some modification, it became the basis for the Mishnah, the fundamental written text of the Talmud.

The work of the Anshei Knesses Hagedolah was complete. They had sealed the Scriptures against falsification and manipulation; they had built protective "fences" around the Torah; they had secured the efficacy of prayer; and they had planted the seeds of the Talmud which would guarantee the preservation of the Oral Law. They had also encouraged the proliferation of *yeshivos* and a broad dissemination of Torah study.[50] The Torah was sinking deep roots in the revived Jewish community in a form designed to weather the unpleasant surprises the future so often brings. The future seemed assured.

Just one thing remained to be done. One of the salient features of the first thousand years of Jewish nationhood had been the battle against pagan influences. The annals of the Periods of the Judges and the Kings chronicle with almost dismal monotony the ebb and flow of this incessant struggle for spiritual survival. Indeed, the Talmud intimates that the idolatrous influences were so powerful in ancient times that even the sages of the Talmud would have been hard-pressed to resist.[51] This burning issue now faced the Anshei Knesses Hagedolah. How could the Jewish people be protected from the terrible trap of idolatry that had ensnared generations closer in time to the Revelation at Mount Sinai? What good were all the "fences" and reinforcements to Judaism if the people remained vulnerable to the siren's call of idolatry?

This problem had troubled the leading sages of all earlier generations, and their solution had been to fire the national zeal, to strengthen the adherence to the Torah and its commandments, to "seek God" in every aspect of life. Bitter experience, however, had shown that such levels of intensity could not be maintained indefinitely, that revivals were almost always followed by relapses. And although the relapses were eventually followed by new revivals, each relapse took a horrendous toll of the Jewish people.

The Anshei Knesses Hagedolah understood that the debilitated Jewish community, subservient to pagan masters, was too fragile to withstand the violent pendular swings that had characterized the days of independence. In desperation, they resorted to drastic measures that had never been contemplated by the sages of earlier generations.

As the Talmud relates, the Anshei Knesses Hagedolah beseeched God to remove the human inclination to idolatry, to lobotomize that part of the human psyche so to speak; at the same time, they also considered the removal of the libidinous inclination, but they realized that to do so would bring an end to procreation.[52] This brief passage in the Talmud, which draws a parallel between the inclination to idolatry and the libidinous inclination, sheds tremendous light on the entire Biblical period.

The human psyche is composed of many drives and impulses, some of which are logical and some of which are not. For instance, hunger and thirst, which seek to replenish vital stores of the body, are logical drives. The libidinous drive, however, has no logical rationale, and if it did not exist, it would be difficult for a person to fathom that such a thing were possible. Nonetheless, God instilled this instinct in people so that they would procreate and the survival of the species would be assured.

Some impulses, such as the acquisitive impulse, may seem logical at first glance but are actually not. One might think that, since people need material things to survive, it is reasonable for a person to accumulate as much material wealth as he can. But people driven by the acquisitive impulse are inclined to accumulate far more than they will ever need. "One who loves money," Solomon writes in *Ecclesiastes*, "is never sated with money."[53] In other words, the passionate desire for material possessions is an illusion. The greatest exhilaration of the acquisitive experience is undeniably in the anticipation and the first brief period of possession. Then the thrill is gone; the satisfaction of the chase is dissipated by its fulfillment. If the object of the chase had been something of substance, however, surely the fulfillment should have been sweeter than the chase.

We must conclude, therefore, that the acquisitive impulse, like the libidinous, is an illogical instinct instilled in people by God to stimulate the growth of civilization. And like the libidinous impulse, it is a constructive force if channeled properly and a destructive force if uncontrolled.

In ancient times, there was another human instinct which we may call the devotional impulse. This potent drive was instilled by God in people to facilitate enhanced states of spirituality. But like the other impulses, it was a dangerous tool. Properly channeled, it could bring a person very close to God. But if a person lacked discipline and character, it could drag him into wanton idolatry. The devotional impulse, misdirected towards idolatrous worship, could then become a compulsive obsession comparable to libidinous and acquisitive obsessions that we find easier to understand. How else can one explain the Canaanite practice of child sacrifice? Would a mother or father in our own times throw a child into the flames to feed a hungry god? Clearly, these ancient pagans were driven by powerful psychic forces that we cannot fathom because they no longer exist.

The Anshei Knesses Hagedolah had done away with the devotional impulse, but there was a heavy price to pay. Never again would the Jewish people be plagued by the cancer of idolatry, but never again would they equal the transcendent spirituality of the core element during the Biblical period. The prophets and sages of earlier times were undoubtedly as capable as the Anshei Knesses Hagedolah of effecting the removal of the devotional impulse, but they chose not to do so. The devotional impulse was too precious a tool to relinquish. But times had changed, and in the opinion of the Anshei Knesses Hagedolah, the risks of keeping it were simply too great.[54]

Thus fortified by the phenomenal work of their venerable sages, the Jewish people entered into a new phase of their history. No longer could they communicate with God through His prophets. No longer did they have an independent kingdom to champion the immortal ideals of the Torah. No longer could they bask in the reflected glory of the Davidic kings. But they had the Torah and they had the land and they had the rebuilt Temple, and for the time being, it was more than enough.

The catharsis of the Babylonian conquest had helped them recover their bearings, and now, they were once again on the road to the fulfillment of its destiny. But a new nemesis lurked over the horizon. A thousand miles to the northwest, a new world power was emerging on the Greek peninsula in southeastern Europe.

The Greeks also sought to achieve a state of expanded spirit and mind, but their approach was so contrary to the Jewish approach that coexistence was clearly out of the question. The Greeks and all they stood for would henceforth become the implacable adversary of the Jewish people for all future history, changing form in subtle ways that could not have been imagined at the time.

8

The Rise of the Greeks

> *O Lord! Do not keep still . . . for your enemies are shouting, and your foes have raised up their heads.*
>
> *(Psalms 83:2-3)*

At the time the Jewish people were establishing an idealistic society based on the sublime Torah, when the cities of Mesopotamia were thriving centers of commerce and culture, when the sophisticated, dynastic kingdom of Egypt was already ancient, nomadic barbarian tribes still roamed the forests and plains of the European continent. There were no cities, no commerce, no agriculture, no crafts, no literature, no legal systems, no kingdoms, just a vast cultural wasteland. But on the Greek peninsula at the extreme southeastern corner of Europe, the first stirrings of a primitive civilization were just beginning to appear.

The early Greeks, a conglomeration of successive waves of barbarian migration, were descended from Yavan, a grandson of Noah; the ancient Hebrew name for Greece is Yavan, which derives from the Hebraic rendering of Ionians, the principal Greek tribe.[1] The first Greek settlers were an illiterate people who left no written record for posterity, but the form into which

Greek society evolved, as well as archaeological excavations and the literature of the later periods, sheds some light on its genesis.

Ancient Greek society was very much a product of its geography. Unlike the broad expanses of the Mesopotamian plains and valleys crisscrossed by overland trade routes and broad navigable rivers, Greece is a forbidding land of rugged mountain ranges, deep valleys and turgid streams. It enjoys a temperate Mediterranean climate, but the rocky soil is not well-suited for agriculture. Nevertheless, the barbarian tribes who migrated to Greece found it a quite desirable environment. They pitched their camps in the isolated valleys, protected by reasonably defensible mountain barriers and passes. Moreover, being of nomadic origin, they did not have much interest in agriculture. Their simple needs were met by the teeming forests, which provided ample game for hunting, and the rock-strewn hillsides, which provided ample pastureland for their livestock.

With the passage of time, the Greeks built fortified villages in the places where their ancestors had pitched their crude camps, and they appointed kings to govern them. But with poor transportation and communications, the isolation of the settlements prevented the emergence of a national state in the manner of the Near Eastern models prevalent at the time. Instead, the Greeks formed numerous, fiercely independent city-states that constantly fought with each other when they were not joined together in loose confederations against a common danger. Culturally, however, there was a kind of unity among the Greeks. They had similar lifestyles and forms of government, spoke the same language and worshipped the same gods.

As the Greeks moved away from their barbarian customs and took on the trappings of civilized life, the growing settlements could no longer subsist on hunting and animal husbandry. They turned to agriculture and, for a time, became a predominantly agrarian society, but the infertile Greek soil, unlike the lush soil of Egypt and Mesopotamia, could not support a higher civilization. Again, geography dictated the next step, and the Greeks turned to the sea.

As it turned out, the sea indeed held the key to the future of

the Greeks. The long, irregular coastline of the Greek peninsula, punctuated by numerous bays and gulfs, provided many
natural harbors within easy access of most of the city-states. The
first hardy Greeks that ventured out onto the sea did so for the
purpose of piracy, preying on the trading ships that plied the
Mediterranean trade routes. But along with their ill-gotten
booty, they also brought back new ideas and attitudes and a
more sophisticated view of the world. The Greeks had discovered civilization.

It did not take long for the Greeks to realize that, in the long
run, trade was a far more lucrative pursuit than piracy. They
built trading fleets and a strong navy to protect them, and they
began to transport merchandise from one port of call to another, realizing considerable profit in the process.

As Greece became a maritime power and the Greek cities
flourished and prospered, the Greeks entered into a period of
territorial expansion. At first, they colonized the Cyclades Islands, a five-hundred-island archipelago in the Aegean Sea off
the eastern coast of Greece, and from there, it was but a short
step into Asia Minor, where Greek settlements were established
along the western coast.

This phase of Greek expansion was not a concerted effort
among the various Greek city-states. Rather, it was accomplished
by a number of the more powerful city-states acting indepen-
dently and in their own interests, but the cumulative effect was
that entire rim of the Aegean Sea was absorbed into the Greek
political patchwork of the time. The principal colonizers among
the Greek peoples were the Dorians, whose principal city was
Sparta in the region of Lacedaemonia, and the Ionians, whose
principal city was Athens in the region of Attica; the Ionians
would eventually become the dominant Greek people. Almost
invariably, however, the colonies soon broke free, forming independent city-states with only a cultural kinship to their mother
cities.

Greece was well on its way to becoming an important member of the civilized world, but then catastrophe struck. Beginning in about 1100 b.c.e., a tidal wave of barbarian migration,
perhaps the same as destroyed the advanced civilization of
Crete, swept over the Greek peninsula and ravaged it. Greek

society slipped into a dark age, reverting to more primitive forms and losing contact with the outside world. For well over a century, Greece licked its wounds, but when it finally reentered the civilized world it was with a force and vitality that far surpassed anything previously displayed.

Once again, the Greeks built ships and ventured out onto the sea. This time, however, in addition to material wealth, they brought back the Phoenician alphabetical writing, adding vowel sounds to accommodate their own melodious language. If the pen is indeed mightier than the sword, then a tremendous weapon had been placed in their hands, a weapon they would use to devastating effect.

In about 800 b.c.e., at about the same time that Solomon was ascending the throne of the Kingdom of Israel, a Greek teller of folk tales named Homer appeared on the stage of history. Using the new art of alphabetical writing, he composed the *Iliad*, an epic poem describing the Greek conquest of Troy in 1184 b.c.e., and the *Odyssey*, its sequel.

MAP II

The Greek Heartland

Troy, or Ilium as the Greeks called it, was an important city in Asia Minor. The heroic siege and conquest of Troy was, in all likelihood, a highlight of the colonization campaigns of the early Greek period, and for centuries, it had been a favorite subject of storytellers. With the constant telling and retelling of the story, many embellishments from popular myth and legend were added, and by the time it reached Homer's times, the story had grown to enormous proportions. In order to preserve the highly detailed story for posterity, or perhaps for some other reason, Homer decided to put down the story in writing, undoubtedly adding many embellishments of his own in the process.

According to the Homeric story, a Trojan prince named Paris carried off the fair Helen, wife of Menelaus, King of Sparta. In outrage, a group of petty Greek kings, headed by Agamemnon, King of Mycenae and brother of Menelaus, organized an expedition to recapture Helen and take vengeance upon the Trojans. The climactic events described in the *Iliad* are set in the tenth and final year of the siege of Troy. The cast of characters is almost equally divided between members of the human race and members of the god race; the line of demarcation between the human race and the god race is further blurred by some characters who are offspring of cohabitation between humans and gods. All these characters maneuver and fight against each other on and off the battlefields, and the result is a sweeping tale of bravery, prowess, courage, cowardice, loyalty, passion, treachery, adultery, pride, greed, honor and disgrace.

Homer's story was a work of genius, a literary masterpiece remarkable for its style, poetic forms, imagination, characterization and close examination of the human experience in the realm of the gods. Indeed, it was such a rich mother lode of literary material that it formed the basis for much of future Greek and Roman literature, most notably the works of Aeschylus and Euripides, Greek tragedians of later periods, and Vergil, the leading Roman dramatist. The *Iliad* has come to be recognized as the first outstanding work in the history of secular literature, for although the gods figure prominently in the story, the poem was never considered sacred writing in any way.

Homer had created a new, written art form, and although there was also artistry in oral storytelling, the structured composition of the written poem was a superb new creation, an enduring work of art.

But even more than inaugurating a distinguished literary tradition, the *Iliad* had a profound although exquisitely subtle impact on Greek society, an impact that was probably not fully appreciated at the time. Until then, the Greeks had lived under the subjugation of the imaginary god race, much in the manner of Mesopotamia, Egypt and most other societies of the ancient world. Homer's works, however, implanted the germ of a new thought in the Greek mind. Although the god race was certainly more powerful than the human race, which of the two was actually superior? Had the gods ever written a poem? Had they built beautiful buildings? And who had decided what the gods did or said in the seminal legends of the Trojan War through which the gods were known to the people? Was it the gods themselves, or was it Homer, the human manipulator of the gods?

It began to dawn on the Greeks that Homer had captured the gods and imprisoned them in his epic poem, establishing once and for all that the most wondrous inhabitant of the earth was man, with his daring, his inventiveness and his creative genius. Of course, man still had to appease and accommodate the gods in order to avoid their deadly fury, but that did not make man inferior to the gods. Rather, it was as if the human race was living among dangerous wolves; prudence would certainly require the humans to do everything necessary to prevent the wolves from attacking, but the humans would still be unquestionably superior to the wolves. And thus, the Greek members of the human race stood poised to assume the mantle of supremacy from the god race.

In its infancy, this radical new idea was little more than a subliminal feeling, but it quickly sank roots into the rocky Greek soil. The next two centuries saw the Greeks emerge gradually from under the thumb of the god race and drink deeply of the wine of freedom.

Until then, the typical king of the Greek city-state had ruled by the authority of his alleged descent from Zeus, "the father of gods and heroes," and although he traditionally consulted with the tribal chieftains and nobles, the king was the supreme military commander, chief magistrate and high priest. In the post-Homeric period, however, the independent spirit of the little city-states was increasingly channeled into a newfound desire for political rights and freedoms, and the role of the kings went into sharp decline.

In one city-state after another, wealthy landowners seized power and restricted the kings to ceremonial and religious functions, but aristocratic rule did not last. Pressure from merchants and the lower classes resulted in the emergence of enlightened tyrants who deposed the aristocrats and enacted reforms. They taxed the aristocrats, stimulated trade and manufacturing, patronized the arts and spent lavishly on civic beautification projects which employed the poor. Ultimately, the tyrants were themselves overthrown, and a system of elections and limited government spread across the land.

The Greek city-states had prepared themselves to become masters of their own destiny, but their destiny proved exceedingly difficult to master. With new governments sensitive to the needs of all the people, the city-states became attractive places to live, and foreigners and Greeks from outlying districts streamed into the cities, swelling their populations to the point of crisis.

The governments reacted by restricting citizenship and the right to vote to those whose parents had been citizens. Protecting the precious privileges of the citizens, however, was not enough to make the hungry underclass disappear. Some pressure was relieved by a new wave of colonization that spawned independent daughter cities across the northern rim of the Mediterranean basin, the most important being Byzantium in Asia Minor, Marseilles in what is now France, Syracuse on the island of Sicily and Naples (Neapolis) in southern Italy, which came to be called Greater Greece (Magna Graecia). For the most part, however, the Greek city-states responded to their internal pressures by warring with each other constantly, either individually or in ever shifting regional alliances.

Slowly but inexorably, the city-states of Sparta and Athens emerged as the principal contestants for the Greek soul. In

Sparta, the principal city of the Dorian Greeks, the liberated spirit of man was poured into a collective mold. Man could free himself from the domination of the gods, but only as part of a monolithic state, a whole which was greater than the sum of its parts. The affairs of state were technically in the hands of all hereditary citizens who chose a representative assembly, but the actual decisions on all matters of importance were made by a five-man council with dictatorial powers.

Military power was the ideal towards which Spartan society strived. All male citizens were drafted during childhood and trained to be obedient cogs in the state military machine that controlled their lives, while the disenfranchised majority of the population labored as serfs to support the soldier-citizens; education was limited almost exclusively to physical training and fighting ability. As a result, Sparta grew strong and began to conquer its neighbors, oppressing and exploiting the captive populations, until most of the Peloponnesian Peninsula in southern Greece was under its dominion.

Athens, the principal city of the Ionian Greeks, went in the opposite direction. Athens became a center of free enterprise and robust economic growth in which individualism was encouraged and nurtured, although the system of limited representation still favored the aristocracy.

In 721 b.c.e., a reformer by the name of Draco codified and

MAP 12

The Greek Expansion

recorded Athenian law for the first time, thereby extending protection to all citizens. In 594 b.c.e., Solon enacted further reforms, including the abolishment of debtor enslavement. In 546 b.c.e., Pisistratus instituted land reform, breaking up the great estates and giving more citizens economic independence. And in 508 b.c.e., Cleisthenes reorganized the government, creating a popular assembly of all the citizens which convened monthly to vote on all legislation and policy. Under this system of full and direct democracy, Athens became the richest city-state in Greece, a thriving commercial and cultural center with a strong navy and vital overseas interests, the intellectual capital of the entire Greek world.

But while the Greek city-states sought their own destiny in the isolation of their mountainous peninsula, the rising power of the Persian kingdom spread into Asia Minor, overwhelming the Greek city-states along the western coast. The Persians then pushed across the Dardanelles into Europe, seizing control of Thrace, a semi-barbaric land roughly corresponding to present-day Bulgaria. The Persians were on the doorstep of Greece, but for decades, the mighty Persian colossus and the apprehensive European Greeks eyed each other warily without resorting to war.

In the conquered Greek cities of Asia Minor, however, accustomed as they were to the new political freedoms, the Persian yoke proved unbearably oppressive, and unrest seethed along the western coast. Finally, in 499 b.c.e., the district of Ionia, which had originally been colonized by Athenian settlers, revolted against Persia with the support of Athens and Eretria on the mainland. The Ionian revolt was crushed in 494 b.c.e., but for the Persians, it was the last straw. The intervention of the mainland Greeks was intolerable. There was no choice but to vanquish this upstart European rival.

The first Persian assault on the Greek mainland was a seaborne punitive attack directed at Athens. In 490 b.c.e., a Persian fleet landed an army near Marathon on the coast of Attica and prepared to march on Athens. The Athenians appealed to the other city-states for help, but because of inter-Greek squabbling, none was forthcoming. Nonetheless, the Athenian army was able to defeat the Persians on the battlefield and win a temporary respite from Persian imperial pressure.

For the next ten years, both sides prepared for the inevitable second round. With its prestige immeasurably enhanced by the military victory at Marathon, Athens was able to rally the other cities around its banner. At a congress in the city of Corinth, Athens, Sparta and many other cities agreed to set aside their differences and form a defense league against Persia.

In 480 b.c.e., a Persian army crossed Asia Minor into Thrace and marched through Macedonia and Thessaly towards the heart of the Greek mainland. At the same time, a large Persian fleet stationed itself off the coast of Attica to provide military support and provisions for the Persian land forces. A small Spartan squadron tried to block the Persians at the mountain pass of Thermopylae, but the Persians overwhelmed the Spartans and flooded into central Greece. Athens was evacuated just before the Persians captured and laid waste to the city.

But the battle was not over. The Athenian navy dealt the Persian fleet a crippling blow near the island of Salamis off the coast of Attica, forcing it to return to Asia. Without the support of its fleet, the Persian army suffered a crushing defeat at the hands of a combined Greek force at Plataea. The Persian army withdrew in disarray from Europe, and the Ionians in Asia Minor seized the opportunity to revolt again. The combined Greek forces then pursued the retreating Persians, and by 478 b.c.e., the Greek cities in Asia Minor had been liberated.

The Greek forces had won a glorious victory. The Persian presence had been completely removed from the Aegean area, and the Greeks had established themselves as a formidable power in the arena of world affairs. The greatest beneficiary by far of the Greek victory was Athens, which emerged as the dominant power on the peninsula, converting the defense league by force of arms into an Athenian regional empire and imposing its own democratic political system and cultural institutions on the other cities under its control.

Intoxicated with its new aura of invincibility, Athens embarked on a golden age in which the cultural seeds planted by Homer centuries before finally came into full harvest. Under the leadership of Pericles, the riches of the Athenian empire were poured into architectural projects, such as the Acropolis and the Parthenon, and the patronage of the arts. Greek literature, which had been largely restricted to epic and lyric poetry, began to develop new forms. The art of drama was born with the tragedies of Aeschylus, Sophocles and Euripides and the comedies of Aristophanes, many of which borrowed heavily from the Homeric themes of the Trojan War. Sculpture entered into a new phase of exquisite grace and perfection that virtually deified the human form.

Eminent thinkers, such as Socrates, Plato and Aristotle, abandoned mythological explanations of the universe and searched within the expanding boundaries of the human mind for the answers to the paramount questions of existence and reality. Philosophical inquiry spilled over into an examination of the natural world, leading to remarkable advances in mathematics and science and the growing conviction that the onslaught of the human intellect was irresistible. Man was indeed the true master of the world; nothing stood higher than human creativity and human intelligence.

In spite of the new intellectual sophistication, however, the god race managed to survive as an integral part of Greek society. The festivals, the folklore, the social customs, the religious beliefs of the lower classes were so intimately entwined with the mythological hierarchy that to abandon it would have unsettled the entire social order.

Even the philosophers, who discerned and discussed the concept of a Supreme Being, continued to give lip service to the god race, although Greek philosophers as early as Xenophanes were already whispering that the gods were myths. It is possible that some of them did harbor a residual belief in the god race, it was undoubtedly only as a remote possibility of little significance, much as a modern day scientist might avoid the rumored habitats of the Loch Ness monster or the Abominable Snowman or any other popular bugaboo undeserving of scientific investigation when matters of greater importance demanded attention. Thus, it was socially and intellectually expedient to allow the god race to cavort in ignorant bliss while the brilliant minds of superior man probed the expanding horizons of human knowledge.

Once again, the literature of the Greeks reveals their true attitude towards the god race. In a telling passage from one of the popular comedies,[2] the god Dionysus and his human slave Xanthias exchange costumes, causing confusion as to who is the god and who is the slave. It is decided to determine the truth by whipping each one. When they both cry out in pain, other methods are sought, and Dionysus ruefully comments that it would have been a good idea to have thought of the alternate method before the whipping was administered. Clearly, reverence for the gods had been replaced by ridicule and condescension; the mythological gods had been demoted to social mascots indulged and patronized by their human masters.

Man had become the new god race in the Greek mode of thought. Man was immortal, collectively if not individually; moreover, according to Plato the only true reality lay in the idea behind material things, and therefore, everything was immortal through its idea. Man had the creative genius to produce superlative literature, art and architecture; the spectacular temples and statues of the gods glorified the human race, not the god race. Man, with his intellectual faculties, could smash any barrier more effectively than the lightning bolts of some Olympian deity.

And thus, man stood alone at the pinnacle of creation. The Supreme Being discerned by the philosophers was viewed as a distant Primal Cause with no active involvement or interest in earthly affairs, and the god race, if it actually existed, was nothing more than a group of overgrown, self-indulgent brutes. Man had no rivals for supreme mastery of the earth, and he alone deserved to be adored and worshipped. The Greeks had become their own gods, and they worshipped themselves with all their hearts and souls.

The brilliant talents of the Greeks, however, did not extend to the political arena. Despite their artistic and scientific achievements, the Greek city-states could not discover the key to peaceful coexistence. Athens continued to exert its power and influence with a heavy hand, and the other cities, deprived of their cherished independence, grew increasingly resentful of Athenian hegemony. Sparta, with the support of Corinth, fanned the hot flames of jealous hatred and plotted to undermine

Athenian military power, sparking the outbreak of the Peloponnesian Wars in 431 b.c.e.

For twenty-seven years, the fortunes of war shifted back and forth between Athens with its naval supremacy and Sparta with its superior land forces, and in the process, the heartland of Greece was ravaged and devastated. Ultimately, the balance was tipped in favor of Sparta when Persia, which was still engaged in sporadic skirmishes with Athenian forces in Asia Minor, sent ships and money to support the Spartan cause. Athens was defeated, and the Athenian regional empire collapsed.

In the aftermath of the Peloponnesian Wars, Sparta emerged as the dominant power of Greece in 404 b.c.e., but the militaristic Spartan hegemony lasted a mere thirty years. Thebes, with the support of Corinth and Athens, formed a coalition that crushed the Spartans and introduced a period of Theban hegemony in 371 b.c.e., at about the time when the Medes and the Persians were conquering Babylon and establishing the Persian Empire in Mesopotamia. In 362 b.c.e., a coalition led by Athens and Sparta defeated Thebes and plunged Greece into another period of incessant intercity warfare, exhaustion, chaos and anarchy, with no end in sight.

Greece was ripe for conquest, but the conquerors came from an unlikely direction. Imperial Persia, still smarting from the defeats of the previous century made no moves toward a new campaign against Greece. North of the Greek peninsula, however, in the kingdom of Macedonia, a vigorous new power was taking form beyond the notice of the distracted, warring Greek cities. Macedonia was a culturally backward but well-organized country, united under the ambitious leadership of Philip II. With consummate diplomatic skill, lavish bribery and judicious military intervention, Philip annexed one city after another until most of the Greek mainland was under his control.

In a desperate effort to avert total Macedonian domination, the Athenian leader Demosthenes organized an alliance against Philip, but in 338 b.c.e., the disciplined and well-trained Macedonian army destroyed the Athenian alliance. After twenty years of clever maneuvering, Philip of Macedonia was the undisputed master of Greece.

Philip was a passionate admirer of Greek culture, and his conquest of Greece was motivated as much by a desire to preserve Greek cultural accomplishments as by his own personal ambition. With his customary cleverness, he welded the Greek cities into a single state with a unified army and navy, a culturally superior and militarily invincible state capable of defeating the Persian Empire and assuming the leadership of the entire civilized world. But the Macedonian king did not live to see his global ambitions come to fruition.

In 336 b.c.e., two years after absorbing the whole of Greece into his kingdom, he was assassinated by one of his own soldiers. The next phase of his master plan was left in the capable hands of his twenty-year-old son and successor, who had been nurtured on the Greek modes of thought and had been tutored by Aristotle himself. The new Macedonian king's name was Alexander.

Alexander the Great, as he came to be known, would establish the largest empire of the ancient world, an empire that would penetrate all the way across the Himalaya Mountains into India. And he would plant the seeds of Greek culture in every place he conquered, transforming the world more profoundly than any other imperial conquest ever had or ever would.

At long last, the stage was set for the first direct confrontation between the Greek idea and the Judaic idea, a confrontation that would set in motion the forces of destiny that would thereafter govern world history.

9

First Encounters

Towards the end of fourth century before the common era, at about the time the Second Temple was being built in Jerusalem, Aristotle was bringing Greek civilization to the zenith of achievement. Following in the footsteps of Socrates and Plato, Aristotle investigated philosophy, government, literature, mathematics, physics and the natural sciences. The fruits of his scholarship influenced Western thought for two thousand years, but the style of his thought processes had an even greater impact. Socrates, Plato and the other earlier philosophers and mathematicians had been artists. Aristotle was a scientist.

More than anything else, Aristotle was remarkable for the orderliness of his brilliant mind and the sheer number of directions in which he pointed it. Never one to plunge headlong into the seas of knowledge, he always began with a dissection of the subject under study. He would delineate his objectives, define a set of terms by which to categorize the data he encountered and only then conduct his inquiry. In this way, he formalized logic, developed controlled experimentation and the scientific method of inquiry and compiled veritable encyclopedias of information garnered through observation, analysis and pure speculation. He also formulated numerous terms, such as matter, form, energy, infinity, genus and species, which endure until this day as basic units of Western thought. Above all, Aristotle was a disciplined student with an insatiable appetite for knowledge—of practically any kind.

In Aristotle's system, nothing is spared the scrutiny and manipulation of human reason. Even God's place is designated by reason. God is defined as the ultimate perfection, form without matter, eternal, unchanging,[1] deserving of honor but requiring no praise.[2] Aristotle believed there was intelligent design in the universe, but he recognized no divine revelation that communicated the purpose of that design. God had created the world and then withdrawn from active involvement within it. In the practical world, it was up to human reason to devise codes of ethics and morality for the individual and utopian schemes for governing society with justice and stability.

If Homer's *Iliad* had fired the first shot in the war between humanity and the god race for supremacy on the planet, Aristotle administered the *coup de grace*. More than any other man, Aristotle opened all frontiers of civilized life to the domination of human reason. He was the one who devised the tools and methods by which humanity could claim mastery over the earth and the right to supplant the Olympian deities as the new god race.

But if humanity had assumed the mantle of the god race in the Greek mode of thought, the idealized image of the ultimate man, the "Greek god" so to speak, was not the homely, squint-eyed thinker such as Socrates or Aristotle. For if man was a god then all of him was divine, his body, his mind and his soul. Just as, in our own times, the crowds cheer the drivers of racing cars rather than the engineers who design them, the adoration of ancient Greek society was reserved for the sun-bronzed, heroic warrior-athlete, his body perfect and beautiful, his mind enriched by philosophy, his soul nourished by literature. The philosophers and writers were admired but not idolized as heroes. They were the engineers who designed the cultural tools, but the true Greek gods were the splendid human sculptures molded by those tools.

Ironically, the man who came closest to the Greek heroic ideal was Alexander the Great, who was not even a Greek but a Macedonian. Macedonia was a backward country of hardy mountainfolk that in all of antiquity did not produce a single philosopher, scientist, thinker, writer or artist whose name is known to history. But its ambitious king, Philip II, was an ardent admirer of Greek culture, and he hired the best tutors to give his gifted son Alexander the benefits of a first-class Greek upbringing. Among others, the illustrious Aristotle was brought to the Macedonian capital of Pella to help mold Alexander's mind during his teenage years. Philip himself trained the boy in the arts of war.

Alexander thus became a potent blend of Macedonian toughness and Greek intellect liberally seasoned with the overpowering personal ambition he inherited from his father. Alexander was a superb physical specimen, a ferocious and tireless warrior, a lover of Greek culture who carried Homer's *Iliad* with him on his campaigns and kept it under his pillow at night next to his dagger, a man with a kingdom at his command and the dream of a world empire in his heart. Alexander was a man cast in the true mold of the Greek hero, and as we trace the progress of his career from its meteoric rise to its tragic end, we find that it mirrors the parabolic course of the Greek civilization from which it sprung.

Alexander ascended the Macedonian throne in 336 b.c.e. at the age of twenty following the assassination of his father Philip. Philip had forced the warring Greek states into a confederation under his leadership, and he was preparing to cross into Asia and attack the Persian Empire when he met his untimely death. The task now fell to his young son.

At first, it seemed that Philip's hard-earned gains would not survive his death. The barbarian tribes in the northern provinces of Thrace and Illyria immediately revolted, while in the capital of Pella, factionalism and conspiracies were the order of the day. At the same time, a number of Greek city-states renounced their allegiance to Macedonia, and the entire Greek confederation teetered on the brink of disintegration. In Persia, the emperor Darius breathed a sigh of relief as he saw the Macedonian threat evaporating into thin air.

Alexander's response was ruthless and decisive. He crushed all opposition within Macedonia, then he marched north with dizzying swiftness, crossed the Danube River and destroyed the rebel forces. Having secured his base, he marched south into Greece and defeated the armies of rebellious Thebes, sold its inhabitants into slavery and burned the city to the ground, sparing only the temple and the house of the poet Pindar. After the sack of Thebes, all of Greece bowed like a punctured balloon before the victorious Alexander. Returning to Macedonia with the grudging Greek pledges of allegiance but not much more in the way of military support, he prepared to take on the Persian Empire.

Without the active support of the Athenian navy, Alexander could not contend with the Persian fleet on the open seas. Instead, he decided to fight a land war against Persian sea power by devastating the Persian naval bases. In this way, he could eliminate any threat to his supply lines as he pressed into the heart of the Persian Empire. In 334 b.c.e., he crossed into Asia by way of the Hellespont, defeated a large Persian army at Granicus and swept down the coast of Asia Minor, capturing port after port along the way. In 333 b.c.e., an immense Persian army led by Darius tried to intercept the smaller Macedonian force at Issus in Syria, but the Macedonian infantry phalanxes and massed cavalry charges routed the undisciplined Persians. Alexander then proceeded down the coast, besieging and capturing the Phoenician port of Tyre and then Gaza. Egypt, chafing under Babylonian and Persian rule for two centuries, surrendered without a blow towards the end of 332 b.c.e.

The entire coastline of the eastern rim of the Mediterranean Sea now belonged to Alexander. It was a stunning triumph. A council of Greek cities at Corinth voted him a golden crown of victory and, for the first time, offered active military support to Alexander. The smell of conquest was in the air, and the Greeks wanted to share in the spoils.

In the spring of 331 b.c.e., Alexander returned up the coastline to Tyre, passing but a few miles west of Jerusalem but paying it no heed, and marched east across Syria into the heart of Mesopotamia. The Persian Empire was reeling, mortally wounded by Alexander's early victories, but Darius nevertheless assembled yet another motley host to stand against Alexander's inexorable advance. The armies met on the plains of Arbela not far from the ruins of the Assyrian capital of Nineveh. Once again, the disciplined Macedonian forces, this time reinforced by Greek cavalry, crushed the Persian army, which scattered in disarray. Darius fled north to Media, where he was killed by his officers. The Persian Empire had ceased to exist for all practical purposes.

Unopposed, Alexander marched on to Babylon, which accepted Macedonian rule with equanimity as yet another of the regular changes in rulership. Then he continued east and captured the Persian capitals of Susa and Persepolis in 330 b.c.e. Four short years after the Macedonian invasion, the defeat of Persia was complete.

The vast lands, the cities, the overflowing royal treasuries all fell into Alexander's hands like overripe fruit. The young Macedonian king had become ruler of the entire Imperial Quadrant, and numerous peoples of whom Alexander had

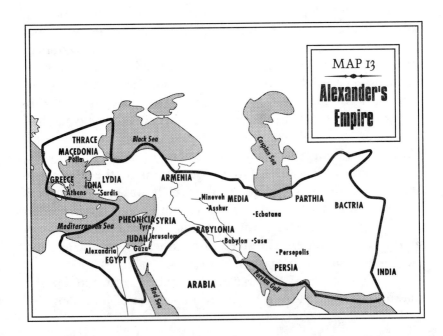

never even heard—the Jewish people most probably among them—had suddenly become his subjects.

True to his upbringing, Alexander planted the seeds of Greek culture among the sundry peoples of his new empire. Greeks colonists followed in the wake of his armies and built Greek cities all along the Mediterranean coastline and throughout Syria and the Tigris-Euphrates valley. Greek culture spread through the conquered lands like an alluring tide, captivating the captive peoples with the grace of its art and architecture, the passion of its dramas, the cleverness of its scholars, the excitement of its athletic games and the siren call to humanity to break the shackles of the god race and breathe the heady air of freedom. In the lexicon of historians, this process was called Hellenization, literally conversion to the culture of Hellas, the Greek name for the mainland of Greece. But the upper classes of the former Persian Empire did not have to be coaxed much to accept Hellenization; the seeds of Greek civilization found Asian soil very fertile.

One gets the impression that Alexander would have been happier had the war against Persia taken forty years instead of four, that he would have been more fulfilled had he spent the best years of his life on the battlefield pursuing glorious dreams of victory. But fate dealt unkindly with him, and at the age of twenty-four, he was already the ruler of a world empire; the prospect of directing the tedious process of Hellenization did not stir the blood in his veins.

Alexander was not a great statesman-general like Napoleon, for whom the challenge of building a universal European state was more thrilling than the clash of armies on the battlefield; one can be reasonably certain that had Napoleon been successful in his Russian campaign he would not have pressed on to conquer China and India! Alexander, on the other hand, was little more than a callow youth with a natural genius for war, a political dilettante who lacked knowledge, sophistication or even interest in statecraft or any of the other sober pursuits of grown men in power. He was a frustrated conqueror, a warrior with no wars to fight.

It is not surprising, therefore, that after a brief period of celebration in Persepolis, Alexander was already seeking new frontiers, new battles, new lands to vanquish. But there were no compelling strategic reasons for choosing any particular direction. A brief survey of the known world beyond the Imperial Quadrant at the time of Alexander reveals a few insular regional powers, many insignificant little countries and shifting streams of nomadic barbarian tribes.

To the east, a patchwork of tribal kingdoms stretched from Samarkand to the Indian Ocean in a long swath encompassing modern-day Turkestan, Afghanistan and Pakistan. Further to the southeast, the sweltering subcontinent of India, a jumble of disunited cities and principalities, contemplated life with the lethargy induced by its torrid climate and the serene passivity fostered by its dominant religions, Buddhism and Hinduism.

In the far distant east, beyond the all but impenetrable barriers of the Tibetan mountains and the Malay jungles, the fabled but rarely seen Chinese Empire was still suffering through its Age of Confusion under the Chow dynasty; the thousands of city-states in the valleys of the Yangtze, Huang-Ho and Yellow Rivers were in a state of chaos and perpetual internecine warfare, while hordes of barbarian Huns exerted intermittent pressure on the Manchurian borders.

To the north, Mongolian and Nordic tribes, crude and uncivilized peoples, roamed the endless steppes of Scythia, the site of modern-day Russia. It would be centuries before demographic pressures would drive them southward and westward towards the heartland of the Imperial Quadrant.

To the south of Egypt and Mesopotamia, the reclusive kingdom of Ethiopia and the pagan tribes of Arabia sat astride both sides of the Red Sea and prospered from the maritime trade with faraway markets across the Indian Ocean.

To the west of Egypt, the Phoenician daughter city of Carthage, the last remaining stronghold of Canaanite culture, dominated the North African coast. Established during the days of King Solomon, Carthage was notorious for its flagrant practice of child immolation, but it was also a flourishing mercantile center with trading outposts along the coasts of Africa and Spain and in nearby Sicily. Carthage enjoyed the prosperity and security of five hundred years of peaceful trade, and there were no indications that it was inclined to military adventures of any sort.

To the south of Carthage, only the wildest legends about the black peoples in the heart of Africa traversed the storm-tossed sand sea of the Sahara Desert.

As we continue northward from Carthage across Sicily and into the heel of Italy, we encounter the Greek cities of Magna Graecia, such as Syracuse and Tarentum, established centuries before during the periods of Greek expansion. This region marked the western extent of the Alexandrine Empire. Further north, we encounter the embattled city of Rome, situated on seven hills alongside the Tiber River in the central Italian district of Latium. Two centuries earlier, Rome had wrested its independence from the Etruscan kingdom north of the Tiber, but now, savage raids by the Cisalpine Gauls, a barbarian Celtic tribe from the far north of Italy, threatened its very existence. Beyond Italy and the coastal settlements, the forests and marshes of Europe teemed with primitive Celtic and Germanic tribes, but only the more advanced Gauls dared approach the civilized lands.

Clearly, no external powers posed a serious threat to the security of the Alexandrine Empire. Realistically, the dangers of insurrection far outweighed the dangers of invasion, but these did not interest the impatient warrior-king as he prepared for new and frivolous military campaigns beyond the borders of the Imperial Quadrant.

We can only speculate about the actual deliberations that determined the course of the next few years, but it seems clear that there were basically two options to be considered. One called for expanding the eastern end of the empire. The other pointed to the west.

From our distant vantage point, it seems that Alexander would have been better advised to turn west. The western region, much closer to his home bases, could have been overpowered with relatively short supply lines, and because of its long familiarity with the Greeks, it could have been Hellenized without much difficulty. Moreover, the Greek cities of Magna Graecia were like a wedge driven into the entire region from which Greek power and cultural influence could be radiated in all directions. As for the strategic value of the region, the conquest of Carthage and the entire Italian peninsula would have made the Mediterranean Sea into a Greek lake and given tremendous impetus to Greek commerce and industry. With the benefit of hindsight, of course, we also know that had Alexander turned west he would have subjugated Rome and prevented the Roman absorption of the Greek world less than two centuries later.

On the other hand, Alexander may have felt that the western lands were already partially Hellenized, while the lands to the east were virtually ignorant of the Greeks. Furthermore, the eastern lands were more contiguous with Mesopotamia, the historic center of the Imperial Quadrant, and therefore seemed to represent the next logical frontier for the expansion of the Quadrant. And finally, one cannot underestimate the allure of the fabled riches of the east; the west promised long-term economic growth, but the east promised stacks of booty.

In the end, Alexander chose the east. For the next six years, he was absent from his seat of power, fighting many forgettable battles and defeating many unimportant foes. He planted the Greek standard all along the eastern frontier of his empire, conquering Bactria and penetrating India through the Khyber Pass. In northern India, he won a battle over an army equipped with war elephants and then appointed the vanquished king to rule in his name; part of India had been added to his empire, but it meant nothing. At this point, Alexander's men refused to push across the deserts to the Ganges River, and Alexander was forced to abandon any dreams of further conquest.

In all his eastern campaigns, at the cost of many thousands of lives, Alexander had founded a few cities, destroyed a few others and not accomplished much of anything else—besides visiting many exotic places and enjoying many youthful escapades. Alexander was a tourist, with an army as his conveyance.

Upon his return to Persepolis in 324 b.c.e., Alexander found his sprawling empire functioning smoothly under the administrative system inherited from his Persian predecessors; his absence had not even been felt. Alexander had enough of a sense of history to want to leave his imprint as a ruler as well as a conqueror, but the method he chose was so bizarre that one suspects his mind was already becoming seriously unhinged. In one spectacular wedding ceremony, Alexander married the daughter of Darius and ninety of his generals also took Persian brides in a symbolic fusion of the Greek and Persian races; all Macedonian soldiers who had taken Asiatic wives were also rewarded. Demented as this showcase extravaganza seems, Alexander himself must have considered it an inspired act of statecraft.

After this outlandish fusion of the races, Alexander discarded his Macedonian garb and took to wearing the opulent robes of Persian royalty. His bloated vanity found expression in numerous paintings, sculptures and coins which bore his likeness. In all of these, the thirty-two-year-old Alexander is portrayed as a handsome youth with flowing hair and a clean-shaven face; although practically all grown men were bearded, Alexander shaved his beard to preserve his boyish good looks. But not even the mightiest emperor can arrest the march of time, and as his youth and sanity slipped away, Alexander began to drink heavily and quarrel with his friends and companions.

Presently, Alexander declared himself a god and demanded that all Greece recognize him as the son of Zeus. The Greeks cities did not particularly mind granting him this indulgence, since in many ways he was indeed more powerful than the emasculated Olympian deities, but it did not go down well with his Macedonian comrades-in-arms. Tensions in the palace rose. Living more and more in a drunken stupor, Alexander began to exhibit frequent fits of violent rage, during which he killed some of his most loyal men. The mind of the god was disintegrating, and his body was not far behind. In 323 b.c.e., Alexander sickened and died after a prolonged drinking bout in Babylon. He was thirty-three years old.

The Alexandrine Empire, held together by one man for seven years, was divided up among the leading Macedonian generals immediately after Alexander's death. In addition to many minor kingdoms and dominions, four principal divisions eventually emerged—the Ptolemaic Empire, the Seleucid Empire, the Kingdom of Macedonia and Greece and the Kingdom of Pergamum in Asia Minor. Alexander's dreams of a world empire died with him, but the process of Hellenization which he had initiated continued for centuries.

Alexander, for all his shortcomings, was undoubtedly one of

the most important figures in history. His conquests drove the roots of classical Greek culture so deep into the soil of the Imperial Quadrant that they could never again be eradicated. But the patterns of his life also afford us a remarkable insight into the dynamics of achievement.

Ordinarily, people spend the productive years of their lives pursuing their goals, and in most cases, even highly successful people leave at least some parts of their ambitions unconsummated. It is extremely rare for a person to achieve, before the prime of life, the complete fulfillment of his goals to the point where there is nothing left to accomplish. Yet this is exactly what happened to Alexander. Alexander was first and last a warrior, prepared from earliest childhood by his father for a lifetime of conquest, specifically the conquest of the mighty Persian Empire. In actuality, however, it took Alexander only four years to overcome Persia, whereas it had taken his father twenty years to overcome Greece.

The young Alexander, never trained for a peacetime role, had reached the pinnacle of his potential, and his whole life stretched before him devoid of goals and aspirations, with no further hopes of accomplishment and fulfillment. It was a terrifying prospect. In desperation, he tried to prolong his growth period by useless campaigns in the east, but these accomplished nothing. Back in Persia, Alexander was forced to face the reality that there was indeed nowhere left to go and nothing left to accomplish, and his life began to collapse. His declaration of godhood, his dementia, his excessive drinking, his fits of violent rage were all symptomatic of a life that had fallen apart at its core.

Yet why did all this have to happen? Why couldn't Alexander simply have sat back and enjoyed the fruits of his brilliant conquests? The answer to these questions goes to the heart of the human condition.

A human being is by nature a volatile creature, constantly bombarded by myriad thoughts, feelings and experiences that keep him in a perpetual condition of flux. Therefore, he is always either in a state of growth or decline; the buffeting forces of life do not allow him to remain indefinitely on a perfectly level plateau. Thus, when a person ceases to rise, he begins to decline. If a person ceases to rise because age or infirmity have sapped his energies, the decline may be relatively mild; if his innermost impetus is still forward, it will counterbalance his decline. If, however, a person ceases to rise because he no longer discerns any higher ground, if his innermost impetus is spent, his decline is precipitous. In Alexander's case, once the decline began it was steep and irreversible, because there were no unaccomplished goals to restrain his fall.

In view of all this, we begin to perceive a striking similarity between the patterns of Greek civilization and the life of its greatest hero. In its youth, we see Greek art and literature declare the independence of man from the god race. As the culture matures, we observe the idea of mankind as the new god race germinating in the Greek mind. In a great rush of literary and philosophical activity, we see the Greek mind consumed with the idea of the supremacy of human reason, and we see the final proclamation of the Kingdom of Man with the arrival of Aristotle. The distant and unknowable Creator, in the Greek view, had no practical involvement in terrestrial affairs. The Olympian deities, if they existed at all, endured only at the sufferance of man. Man had no rivals as supreme master of the planet.

In the Greek mind, the victory of mankind was complete. Man had made himself master of the world with the brilliance of his mind, and the conquests of Alexander had implanted this concept in the entire Imperial Quadrant. Human reason of the Greek variety now ruled the universe; all that remained was to shine the spotlight of reason on each little piece of the universe, and it would surely yield its secrets. Undoubtedly, it would take a long time to do this, but the victors had the luxury of time.

But soon it began to dawn on the Greeks that by their own criteria they had reached the pinnacle of achievement. They breathed the rarefied air of the mountaintop and wondered where to go from there. Admittedly, scientists could busy themselves in their laboratories indefinitely with the study of nature, but what would stir the blood of the rest of society? What goals remained to excite the human spirit and intellect? What pursuits remained besides self-indulgence and material gratification? Was there intrinsic value and meaning to the life of the new god race, or having reached the summit, were they also doomed to the degeneration and frivolity that characterized the Olympian deities? In what manner and to what purpose should a man live to be worthy of his status as a higher being?

These questions plagued the Greek mind in the generations following Alexander, ultimately sending Greek civilization into its inevitable spiral of decline. The ambitious philosophies of Plato and Aristotle, with their global scope and boundless aspirations, gave way to the decadent philosophies of the Skeptics, Epicureans and Stoics.

Distrusting both the senses and reason, the Skeptics denied the possibility of any knowledge with certainty. The wise man should therefore seek tranquility rather than truth, and since all theories were probably false, he should not bother to combat the popular myths. "Nothing is certain," declared Arcesilaus, a leading Skeptic, "not even that."

Epicurus, however, declared that pleasure is certainly good, and pain is certainly bad. Therefore, the value of everything, from wisdom to sensuality, is measured by the pleasure it delivers and the pain it avoids. According to the materialistic philosophy of Epicurus, there is no higher meaning to life, no gods, no spirituality. Only atoms and space exist. Man is not the product of design but a spontaneously generated piece of matter that has evolved through natural selection. His mind and his soul are forms of matter that die together with the body. All man can do is seek a small measure of happiness during his brief stay on the earth, and the key to happiness is pleasure.

The Stoics also presented a materialistic view, but they believed that there was design in the universe and that God and Nature were one and the same. In fact, the Stoics believed there was so much design that everything was predetermined and there was no free will. Man achieves happiness only by a serene acceptance of the course of Nature and by suppression of his own needs and emotions. The Stoic, therefore, seeks a passive life, and his ideal is perfect apathy, an absence of feeling, which will allow him to achieve perfect peace of mind.

None of these philosophies is particularly godly in outlook. Rather, they reflect the sense of disillusionment that dominated Greek culture in the post-Alexandrine period, the gropings of self-appointed gods who have lost their way.

The stumbling of lost gods also characterizes the art and literature of the times. We see the sculpture that represented the human body in its idealized form, such as *The Discus Thrower*, give way to the realistic disclosures of the life-ravaged *Old Market Woman*. We see literature turn away from social commentary and become stylized and shallow, replacing evocative tragedies and acerbic political satire with the pastoral verse of Theocritus and the genteel parlor farces of Menander. We see the creativity and intellectual vigor of Athens replaced by the pitter-patter of librarians preserving the living works of a dying age. We see a society sliding downhill, fumbling about, like a disoriented Alexander, for a way to justify its self-image.

Paradoxically, this period of cultural decline also produced prodigious strides in Greek science and technology. Euclid established standards of geometry that would endure for two thousand years. Archimedes, the foremost Greek scientist, made breakthrough discoveries in hydrostatics and mechanics. The astronomer Hipparchus devised the system of latitude and longitude and invented trigonometry. The geographer Eratosthenes measured the earth's circumference with uncanny accuracy and suggested that one could reach India by sailing west across the Atlantic Ocean. Theophrastus explored botany and pharmacology, Herophilus investigated anatomy, Erasistratus pioneered physiology and preventive medicine, and a host of others probed dozens of frontiers in the study of the natural world.

Upon reflection, however, there is no paradox whatsoever. In actuality, the surge of science and technology did not occur in spite of the declining culture but because of it.

In a vigorous culture, the talented young intellectual is presented with a number of secular avenues that lead to the ultimate goal of intellectual fulfillment. As a philosopher, he can investigate the meaning of life and the relationship of man to the world around him. As a historian, he can examine the forces that determine the rise and fall of societies. If he is creative, he can probe the depths of the psyche through literature or formulate new artistic visions. As a mathematician, he can explore the interrelationships of numbers and forms. As a research scientist in any number of fields, he can hunt for the secrets of the natural world. As a doctor or an inventor, he can improve the life of his fellow men.

Faced with all these options, the young student must make a choice. Occasionally, this choice is determined by a strong affinity for one particular field; he may love to write or play with numerical calculations. The relative opportunities for financial reward undoubtedly play an important role as well. For the most part, however, students will be drawn to the fields that provide the most intellectual stimulus and satisfaction, to the fields that represent the higher intellectual pursuits.

In this sense, it seems clear that the study of philosophy and similar subjective fields surpasses the study of science. The philosopher is concerned with living, thinking subjects. He contemplates the human mind and soul, and no matter how materialistic his doctrine, he deals with values, aspirations and other matters of the spirit. The scientist, on the other hand, is concerned with the mechanical forces that govern both the animate and the inanimate physical world, and no matter how clever his discoveries, his work contains no determinations of good and evil, no right and wrong, no keys to the meaning of life, no spiritual sustenance.

Furthermore, the chain of reasoning that leads the philosopher to his conclusions has real lasting value; indeed, it may often be more valuable than his final conclusions. The scientist, however, is an intelligent hunter rather than a thinker, and therefore, the investigation that leads the scientist to his discovery has no residual value, except that it may offer clues to a related investigation. The importance of the information the scientist discovers is not measured by the process that led to the discovery, whereas the conclusions of the philosopher live and die by the reasoning that gave birth to them.[3]

Therefore, it would seem that under ideal conditions the young intellectual would be drawn to philosophy rather than science.[4] These ideal conditions existed in Greek society during the times of Socrates, Plato and Aristotle when Greek philosophy reached out to conquer the world of knowledge and Greek culture was still full of vigor and ambition. Had the young Archimedes, for instance, come to Athens when Socrates was teaching philosophy, he would surely have been drawn into its intellectual vortex. But by the time, Archimedes was born, philosophy had degenerated. The teachings of the Skeptics, Epicurians and Stoics did not offer much to excite his interest, and it is small wonder that he sought instead the solid ground of scientific inquiry. Thus, it was actually the cultural decline itself that led to the effusion of science and technology in the post-Alexandrine period.

The pattern repeats itself in modern times. After being buried under an avalanche of Christianity for a thousand years, classical Greek culture was revived during the Italian Renaissance in the fifteenth century. For the next three centuries, the reborn Greek spirit gradually shook itself free of the restraints of Christianity, gathering strength with the passage of time. By the end of the eighteenth century, thinkers such as Voltaire, Rousseau, Locke, Leibnitz and Kant brought the new Greek culture, now called secular humanism, to its peak, much as Socrates, Plato and Aristotle had done two thousand years before.

Having reached its limits, the new Greek culture once again began its inevitable decline. During the nineteenth century, the Greek spirit attempted to prolong its vitality and fire its idealism by turning to liberal and socialist philosophies. But in the twentieth century, these ideologies moved from theory into practice and showed themselves quite useless. By the second half of the twentieth century, secular humanism stood exposed as a bankrupt ideology which could only offer society a hedonistic, narcissistic materialism.

Devoid of thinkers, ideology and spiritual inspiration, secular Western society has moved into a new post-Alexandrine period. There is nothing left to fire the spirits and imaginations of aspiring young intellectuals, and therefore, it is small wonder that would-be philosophers and thinkers are making space shuttles, cellular phones and semiconductors instead. Just as in the post-Alexandrine period, the decline of the modern West has led to tremendous progress in science and technology.

This then was the parabolic pattern which characterized the progress of Greek culture in ancient times and its revived form in modern times—a growing awareness of the human genius, a heady declaration of human supremacy, followed by bewilderment, disillusionment and decline. Thus, the downfall of Greek culture was caused by internal depletion rather than by external assault. The historical progress of Judaism, however, stands in sharp contrast to this pattern.

The cycles of rise and decline that characterized Jewish history were never caused by the exhaustion of the nuclear Judaic spirit; there has never been a time when the Torah itself ceased to provide spiritual sustenance to the core element of the Jewish people. Decay sets in when the ultimate goal is reached, but the faithful Jew climbs a mountain without a pinnacle. He acknowledges God as the Master of the Universe and devotes his life to elevating himself and drawing closer to God, a goal that can never be fully achieved. Judaism, therefore, is an inexhaustible source of new spiritual rewards as each new rung of the endless ladder towards God is climbed, and it never goes into internal decline.

External erosion, however, is an altogether different matter. All human beings, by their very nature, are vulnerable to physical or intellectual enticements, and as we have seen, the Jewish people certainly suffered through periods of corrosion by external influences. Whenever the national zeal in the devotion to the Torah faltered, the weaker elements began to wander. In Biblical times, the Canaanites drew them with offers of wanton pleasures. In modern times, the Enlightenment offered exciting new intellectual ideas. In the post-Alexandrine period, the Greeks offered both.

As the Greek presence in Asia became more and more entrenched, the tug of Greek culture began to be felt in Jewish society. Strings of Greek cities along the Mediterranean coast and along the east bank of the Jordan River drew the curious Jewish youth with the enthrallment of their theatrical presentations, the cleverness of their rhetoricians, the pageantry of their athletic tournaments and the licentiousness of their taverns and dance halls. Greek culture, decaying on the inside but glittering on the outside, drew the innocent Jewish youth with its charms, and Jewish society, glittering on the inside, began to be corroded on the outside.

Nevertheless, the first encounters between the Jews and the

Greeks were fairly cordial. The Talmud relates that the Samaritans petitioned Alexander for possession of the Temple Mount in Jerusalem.[5] The Samaritans, transplanted to Israel by the Assyrians two centuries earlier, were old thorns in the side of the Jewish people. They had failed in their attempts to prevent and then disrupt the reconstruction of the Temple, but having assisted in the siege of Tyre,[6] the Samaritans felt that Alexander would rule in their favor. To counter the Samaritan claim, the Jews sent a delegation led by Simon the Just,[7] who was the High Priest and the last surviving member of the Anshei Knesses Hagedolah. At the sight of the eminent sage, Alexander dismounted and bowed with respect. Then he ruled in favor of the Jews, and to the utter dismay of the Samaritans, he subjected them to Jewish authority.

Afterwards, Alexander returned to Jerusalem with Simon the Just to see the Holy Temple. Impressed by its beauty, he suggested that a statue of him be placed in the Sanctuary. Simon the Just gently dissuaded him from this plan, explaining that images were forbidden in Jewish law. Instead, he offered two more lasting memorials—all male Kohanim born that year would be named Alexander and all contractual dates would be measured from the establishment of the Alexandrine Empire.[8] It was a good bargain for both. The Jews were spared the abomination of a statue in the Temple, and in return, Alexander has become a quite common Jewish name and the dating system, known as *minyan shtaroth*, endured for fifteen hundred years.

The Talmud tells of several other disputes that Alexander settled in the favor of the Jews.[9] Josephus also reports many other favorable enactments for the benefit of the Jews, including the exemption from taxes during the fallow sabbatical year. Apparently, the Jewish people and their venerable sages had made a positive impression on Alexander and the Greeks. As a wise and sober people with very high moral standards, the Jews were certainly deserving of the respect of the Greeks. And for their part, the Greeks could well afford to treat the Jews with deference. As far as they could see, Judea was an insignificant little province, comprising little more than the city of Jerusalem, with absolutely no military capability. What threat did this tiny, reclusive nation pose to the mighty Greeks?

It would be many years before it dawned upon the Greeks that the unassuming Jews were their most dangerous foes, that the Jews were the bearers of a potent ideology whose message would electrify the world. Ultimately, the Jews and their Christian and Muslim imitators would bury Greek civilization for a thousand years. In the meantime, however, the Greeks allowed the Jewish people to pursue their own agendas in benign neglect—as long as they paid their taxes.

List of Maps

Timeline of the Kings

Saul *879-877*		
David *877-837*	**850**	
Solomon, son of David *837-797*		
KINGDOM OF JUDAH		**KINGDOM OF ISRAEL**
Rechavam, son of Solomon *797-780*	**800**	**Yeravam I** *797-775*
Aviam, son of Rechavam *780-777*		**Nadav, son of Yeravam** *775-774*
Asa, son of Aviam *777-736*		**Baasha, assassinated Nadav** *774-751*
		Eilah, son of Baasha *751-750*
	750	**Zimri, assassinated Eilah** *7 days in 750*
		Amri, assassinated Zimri *750-739*
Yehoshafat, son of Asa *736-711*		**Ahab, son of Amri** *739-717*
Yehoram, son of Yehoshafat *711-703*		**Achaziah, son of Ahab** *717-715*
Achaziah, son of Yehoram *703-702*		**Yehoram, brother of Achaziah** *715-702*
Asaliah, mother of Achaziah, daughter of Ahab *702-696*	**700**	**Jehu, assassinated Yehoram** *702-674*
Yoash, son of Achaziah *696-656*		**Yehoachaz, son of Jehu** *674-657*
Amatziah, son of Yoash *656-627*	**650**	**Yoash, son of Yehoachaz** *657-647*

		Yeravam II, son of Yoash *647-607*
		Zechariah, son of Yeravam II *6 months in 607*
Uziah, son of Amatziah *627-591*		Shalum, assasinated Zechariah *1 month in 607*
	600	Menachem ben Gadi, assassinated Shalum *607-597*
Yoam, son of Uziah *591-575*		Pekachiah, son of Menachem *597-595*
Achaz, son of Yosam *575-561*		Pekach ben Remaliah, assassinated Pekachiah *595-574*
Hezekiah, son of Achaz *561-533*		Hosheia ben Eilah, assassinated Pekach *574-556*
	550	Assyrian conquest, population deported, **Kingdom of Israel ceases to exist.** *556*
Menashe, son of Hezekiah *533-478*		
	500	
Amon, son of Menashe *478-476*		
Yoshiahu, son of Amon *476-445*		
	450	
Yehoachaz, son of Yoshiahu *3 months in 445*		
Yehoakim, son of Yoshiahu *445-434*		
Yehoachin, son of Yehoakim *3 months in 434*		
Tzidkiahu, son of Yoshiahu *434-423*		
	425	
Babylonian conquest. **Babylonian exile reigns.** *423*		

Notes and Sources

PROLOGUE
THE SEARCH FOR DESTINY

1. *Isaiah* 2:4
2. *Isaiah* 11:9
3. The Messiah will come when the world is totally good or totally evil. (*Sanhedrin* 98a)
4. Rambam, *Teshuvah* 5:5

CHAPTER 1
MODERN TIMES

1. See Prologue.
2. The repeated conquests were themselves a source of expansion, since every conqueror became integrated into the Mesopotamian empire.
3. The city of Babylon, contrary to this pattern, was destroyed by the Persians.

CHAPTER 2
THE BIRTH OF JUDAISM

1. All of these were Canaanite peoples, distant descendants of Canaan, the grandson of Noah; the major tribes were known by their individual names, while the name Canaanite embraced an amalgam of smaller tribes, such as the Refaites, Kaphtorites and Kenizites.
2. Ramban, *Genesis* 45:12
3. *Genesis* 31:47
4. For the most part, the Amorites, Hittites and Jebusites lived in heavily fortified mountain cities, the Hivites were centered around Shechem, Giveon and Mount Hermon, and the Canaanites and Perizites, with cities in the center and the north, lived a nomadic existence, moving from place to place according to the needs of their grazing herds. See Ramban, *Genesis* 13:7.
5. Bab. Tal., *Sotah* 34a
6. Egypt, the prosperous breadbasket along the bounteous Nile River, did not depend upon rainfall for its sustenance. But Abraham's sojourn in Egypt was cut short because of the pharaoh's licentious designs on his wife Sarah.
7. The petty kings of Sodom, Gomorrah, Admah, Zevoim and Bela formed a confederation in rebellion against Kedarlaomer, the Amorite king of Elam in distant

Mesopotamia, to whom they had been paying heavy tribute for a number of years. The insurrection lasted for thirteen years without any retaliation, but in the fourteenth year, King Kedarlaomer invaded Canaan, supported by King Amrafel of Babylon, King Arioch of Elassar and King Tidal of Goim. The Amorite army laid waste to the countryside and routed the mutinous kings in the Valley of Siddim. Sodom and Gomorrah were looted, and Abraham's nephew Lot, who had taken up residence in Sodom, was taken captive. When news of the disaster reached Abraham, he immediately mobilized his considerable forces and attacked the Amorite troops, rescuing his nephew and recovering the captured booty. The exhausted Amorite army withdrew to the outskirts of Damascus, and Canaan returned to its unruly ways.

8. All Jews trace their ancestry to Isaac, while the Arabs trace their ancestry to Ishmael.
9. *Exodus* 33:11
10. *Numbers* 12:3
11. *Hosea* 2:22
12. Bab. Tal., *Makkos* 22b

Chapter 3
The Conquest of Canaan

1. *Deuteronomy* 2:5,9
2. Rashi, *Numbers* 21:1
3. *Joshua* 24:11
4. Jer. Tal., *Sheviis* 6:1
5. ibid.
6. Malbim, *Joshua* 9:1
7. Ibn Ezra, *Ovadiah* 1:20
8. The tribe of Levi, consisting of the Kohanim and the Levites, did not receive a portion; consecrated as a pastoral caste, they were to be supported by an elaborate tithing system mandated by the Torah, and the individual tribes gave them many cities, scattered throughout Israel, as permanent places of residence. The tribe of Simon also did not receive

an individual portion but was given a number of cities within the portion of Judah.
9. All that remained of the former inhabitants in the land of Judah were the Philistine occupants of the Fortress of Yevus in Jerusalem, who were left undisturbed out of respect for the treaty between Abraham and King Avimelech of Philistia centuries before. See Rashi, *Joshua* 15:63
10. *Joshua* 16:10, 17:13
11. *Joshua* 23:6-13
12. *Genesis* 8:21
13. Bab. Tal., *Yevamos* 47a
14. Bab. Tal., *Sanhedrin* 56a
15. *Megillas Taanis*, Epilogue
16. *Joshua* 1:8
17. Meiri, Introduction to *Avos*
18. Bab. Tal., *Zevachim* 119a
19. *Hoshea* 14:3

Chapter 4
Centuries of Troubled Utopia

1. In an effort to rekindle the revolutionary spirit, Mao Zedong gave effective control of the country to the fanatical Red Guards and thereby destroyed the political and intellectual fabric of Chinese society.
2. *Judges* 17:6, 21:25
3. Bab. Tal., *Yevamos* 121b
4. Bab. Tal., *Sanhedrin* 63b. This explains the initial experimentation with idolatry. See discussion at the end of Chapter 7 with regards to the subsequent attractions of idolatry.
5. Ibn Ezra, *Deuteronomy* 33:5
6. *Judges* 3:11. According to *Metzudas David*, based on *Seder Olam*, the forty years of Asniel ben Kenaz include the eight years of oppression.
7. Bab. Tal., *Sukkah* 27b
8. Following the death of Gideon in 1045 b.c.e., there was an abortive attempt by Avimelech, his son by one of his concubines, to establish a monarchy without the sanction of any of the sages or prophets. With the financial support of his mother's

kinsmen in Shechem in the land of Ephraim, Avimelech mobilized a small private army of vagrants and scoundrels. He then proceeded to murder most of his brothers and proclaim himself king. For three years, this brutal despot dominated his unwilling countrymen until he met a violent death during a revolt in his power base of Shechem. The reign of Avimelech was an aberration, and his name does not appear on the king lists of Israel. After his death, the succession of Judges resumed with Tola ben Puah in 1042 b.c.e., followed by Yair of Gilead in 1019 b.c.e.

9. Ivtzan, who came from Bethlehem in the tribal lands of Judah, was also known as Boaz. (Bab. Tal., *Bava Basra* 91a) He married Ruth, the righteous convert descended from King Eglon of Moab. (Bab. Tal., *Nazir* 23b) The story of Boaz and Ruth is chronicled in *The Book of Ruth*. Their great-grandson was King David.

10. He had also served as an auxiliary Judge during the times of Samson.

11. The loss of the Ark, which was far more devastating to the nation than the battlefield defeat at the hands of the Philistines, marked the end of the permanent Sanctuary at Shilo, where it had been for three hundred and sixty-nine years. (Bab. Tal. *Zevachim* 118b) The Mishkan was now returned to Gilgal alongside the Jordan River, where it had been during the War of Conquest in the time of Joshua and where it now resumed the status of a temporary Sanctuary; there would also be brief stays in the cities of Nov and Giveon before the construction of the Holy Temple in Jerusalem during the days of King Solomon.

12. Ralbag, *Judges* 17:6, referring to *Samuel* 7:4

13. Mitzpah stood on the site of the present-day Nebe Samuil.

14. Rashi, *I Samuel* 8:3; *Shabbos* 55b

15. *I Samuel* 12:12

16. Rashi, *Genesis* 49:10

17. The Torah commands, "When you come to the land that God your Lord will give to you, and you conquer it and settle in it, and it shall happen that you will say, 'Let us appoint a king over us, like all the nations around us.' Then you shall surely appoint a king whom God your Lord will choose; you shall appoint the king from among your brethren, but you shall not place above you a stranger who is not your brother." (*Deuteronomy* 17:15-16)

The anomaly of the commandment to appoint a king and Samuel's disapproval of the request of the Elders is the subject of extensive discussion in the commentaries to *Deuteronomy* and to *Samuel* 8:5-6. See *Kli Yakar, Ohr Hachaim,* Ramban and Redak. The resolution presented here, based on the previous discussions, assumes the Ramban's view that the appointment of a king is mandatory rather than optional and follows the general approach of the Redak in explaining why the request of the Elders was inappropriate.

If we look closely at the language of the verses, we see that the people are seeking to choose a political leader. The Ramban explains that this is a prophetic reference to the days of Samuel. "Asimah alai melech kechal hagoim asher sevivosai," they would say (the use of the singular form to represent the plural indicating a united front). "Let us appoint a king over us, like all the nations around us." The Torah responds, however, with a commandment to appoint a king "whom God your Lord will choose," clearly for religious purposes rather than political ones. And since the intent of the people was political it became necessary to stipulate that the king must be Jewish.

CHAPTER 5
THE EXPERIMENT OF THE KINGS

1. In the patriarch Jacob's prophetic designation of the tribal roles over six hundred years before. (*Genesis* 49:10)
2. *Judges* 17:6, 21:25
3. *I Samuel* 9:16
4. "And you shall anoint him as a *nagid* [ruler] over My people, for I have seen the distress of My people whose cries have reached Me ... this one will control My people." (*I Samuel* 9:16) And Samuel said, "Behold, God has anointed you as a *nagid* [ruler] over His estate." (*I Samuel* 10:1)

   In reference to the anointment of David of the tribe of Judah, however, the word *melech*, advice giver, is used. "I will send you to Yishai in Bethlehem, for I have seen among his sons a *melech* [king] for Me." (*I Samuel* 16:1)

   Furthermore, the appointment of Saul as *nagid* is clearly to "control My people ... His estate" The appointment of David as *melech*, however, is "for Me," to fulfill the spiritual designs of God.
5. The concept of *nagid*, of the king as political leader, is introduced at this point in Jewish history, but it remains a recurrent theme throughout the remainder of the Period of the Kings, being used in reference to both the kings of Judah and the kings of Israel. The term *nagid* is not interchangeable with the term *melech*, and a careful study of each usage will invariably reveal its significance within its context.
6. *I Samuel* 10:22-24
7. Redak, *I Samuel* 13:13
8. In the words of Samuel, "You have been foolish in not heeding the command which God your Lord has commanded you, for up to now, God had ordained your kingship over Israel to last *ad olam*, but now, your kingship will not last ..." (*I Samuel* 13:13-14)

   Ad olam, literally, means forever. The Ralbag raises the obvious question: How could the House of Saul have lasted forever if the kings of the tribe of Judah were prophetically preordained? The answer he offers is that in this context it means for a very long time, which is indeed a not uncommon, secondary translation of this phrase.

   In the light of our discussion, it is also possible that, had Saul not faltered, his dynasty would have endured as the political monarchy, and the spiritual monarchy of Judah would have been superimposed over it. At that point, Israel would have enjoyed a two-tiered government, with the administrative duties performed by the House of Saul and the spiritual leadership by the kings of the tribe of Judah.
9. When the tribes came to Hebron to invite David to become king of all Israel, they said, " ... And God said to you, 'You shall shepherd My people Israel, you shall be a *nagid* over Israel.'" (*II Samuel* 5:2) Here we see clearly the dual role of the kings of Judah—the spiritual leader as shepherd and the political leader as *nagid*.
10. For the exact divisions of the authorship of the Psalms, see Bab. Tal., *Bava Basra* 14b.
11. *II Samuel* 23:1
12. Malbim, *I Samuel* 25:1
13. Redak, *II Samuel* 2:11
14. Rashi, *II Samuel* 8:1
15. *I Chronicles* 22:8
16. *II Samuel* 6:16
17. *I Kings* 3:12
18. Rashi, *I Kings* 4:1
19. *II Samuel* 7:12-13
20. *I Kings* 5:5
21. This seems to indicate that they also reached Southeast Asia, to which peacocks are indigenous.
22. Redak, *I Kings* 11:1, quotes this verse from *Jeremiah* 9:22 as referring to

Solomon.

23. *Deuteronomy* 17:17
24. Bab. Tal., *Sanhedrin* 21b
25. Rambam, *Issurei Biah* 13:16
26. Bab. Tal., *Shabbos* 56b
27. *II Kings* 11:4-8
28. Bab. Tal., *Shabbos* 56b
29. Rashi, *Genesis* 25:23
30. Bab. Tal., *Shabbos* 56b; *Sanhedrin* 21b.
The Talmud states that Solomon "married" the daughter of the pharaoh, and indeed, this wording also appears in *I Kings* 3:1. The Talmud in *Yevamos* 76b, however, points out this is merely a euphemistic phrasing, since a traditional nuptial bond with a first generation Egyptian convert is invalid. Therefore, in strict legal terms, there was no marriage, only an exclusive common law relationship which, in Solomon's opinion, was considered acceptable under the circumstances.

CHAPTER 6
KINGDOMS IN DECLINE

1. From the beginning, there was a spirit of rebellion among the restless northern tribes, and therefore, they demanded that the coronation ceremony take place in Shechem in the land of Ephraim rather than in Jerusalem in the land of Judah.
2. Bab. Tal., *Sanhedrin* 102a
3. Redak, *I Kings* 11:26
4. *I Kings* 14:7
5. Bab. Tal., *Sanhedrin* 101b
6. Malbim, *I Kings* 12:28
7. Bab. Tal., *Sanhedrin* 101b
8. However, perhaps we can detect the early signs of a conniving nature even before he became king. The Talmud (*Sanhedrin* 101b) considers it to his great credit that he alone had the courage to raise his voice in protest against Solomon, as described in *I Kings* 11:27. Yet even then, he did not protest the idolatrous practices of Solomon's wives. Rather, he protested that in building palaces for the foreign princesses

Solomon had blocked off some of the access routes to Jerusalem which David had opened for Jewish pilgrims. He did not make the obvious protest against the pagan abominations which the people had greeted with indifference and apathy. Instead, he found an angle of injustice to the people which could be exploited to arouse popular opposition to Solomon. Ironically, he himself would ultimately do far greater injustice to the pilgrims than Solomon had ever done.

9. *Metzudos David, I Kings* 15:6
10. Rashi, *II Chronicles* 11:5
11. *II Chronicles* 11:16
12. *II Chronicles* 12:1
13. *II Chronicles* 12:14
14. *I Kings* 14-22-23
15. The prophet repeatedly reminds us of his mother's identity (see *I Kings* 14:21-31), which the commentators take as an indication that she exerted a strong influence on Rechavam.
16. *Nemukei Yosef*, Bab. Tal. *Bava Kama* 38b.
According to some commentators, Naamah was among the wives of Solomon who reverted to paganism, and she also persuaded Rechavam to turn to idolatry (see Redak and Malbim, *II Kings* 14:21). Rechavam's "abandonment of the Torah," according to these commentators, must therefore be taken literally and in its most extreme sense—idolatry. There are, however, some problems with this view. The prophet tells us (*I Kings* 15:3) that Rechavam was succeeded by Aviam who "repeated all the sins his father had done before him, and he was not as loyal to God his Lord as was his ancestor David." If Rechavam was indeed an idol worshipper, this would mean that Aviam was one as well. Yet in the next few words, the prophet tells us that he was not "as loyal to God as David," the exact words used

in reference to Solomon in *I Kings* 11:4. As mentioned earlier, the Talmud (*Shabbos* 56b) infers from these words that Solomon was certainly loyal and free of sin, but not with the perfect loyalty of David. It follows, then, that whatever the prophet's complaint might have been against Aviam, Aviam was also innocent of actual sin. Furthermore, the account of Aviam in *II Chronicles* 13:3-20 is unreservedly complimentary, and the battlefield speech he delivers is a passionate declaration of loyalty to God; there is absolutely no hint at idolatry or any other sinfulness. It would seem, therefore, that Aviam was a loyal servant of God, albeit with some shortcomings, and if he "repeated all his father's sins," his father Rechavam must have been an equally loyal servant of God. And if his mother was responsible for his upbringing, then she, too, must have been a righteous woman.

Elsewhere, the Talmud (*Bava Kama* 38b) relates that God's solicitude for the safety of Ammon and Moab during the Conquest (*Deuteronomy* 2:5,9) was because of the two "fine fledglings" that would issue from those nations—Ruth of Moab and Naamah of Ammon. If Naamah had relapsed into paganism and dragged down her son, the king of Judah, along with her, she would surely not be considered a "fine fledgling." Once again, the indication seems to be that Naamah was a righteous woman.

Nemukei Yosef in *Bava Kama* makes this observation, as noted above, and concludes that Naamah was indeed a righteous woman and that Solomon's other Ammonite wives were responsible for the worship of Ammonite idols mention in *I Kings* 11: 5-7; the clear indication in *I Kings* 11:1 is that he had indeed married several Ammonite princesses.

Consequently, the entire period

of Rechavam and Aviam must be seen in a different, more positive light. The presentation of the period in these pages follows the reading of *Nemukei Yosef.*

17. Bab. Tal., *Zevachim* 112b
18. Rashi, *I Kings* 14:23
19. *I Kings* 15:12, 22:47
20. *II Chronicles* 14:3
21. *II Chronicles* (14:4) mentions that Asa removed the private altars, but further on (15:17), we are told that the private altars remained. This would seem to indicate that Asa did remove them, but that they kept coming back. As the Talmud notes (*Yoma* 86b), people delude themselves into thinking that their habitual sins are permissible. Certainly, we all know the gravity of the sin of slander, yet how many of us actually refrain from idle gossip? This must also have been the case with the private altars in the Kingdom of Judah. The people had become accustomed to the ease and convenience of the private altars, and therefore, they continued to rationalize and delude themselves.
22. With regards to Baasha, we once again find the use of the term *nagid,* ruler, as a qualification of his role as king, as with Saul and Yeravam. (*I Kings* 16:2)
23. Rashi, *I Kings* 16:23
24. Ralbag, *I Kings* 16:31
25. Redak, *I Kings* 16:31
26. *I Kings* 19:18. This is one of the few places in the Prophets where we get a statistical reading of the extent of spiritual corruption. In *II Kings* 10:18-25, we are told that Jehu convened "all the Baal worshippers" in the temple of the Baal in Shomron, and he had them all killed. This would seem to indicate a far smaller number of Baal worshippers. However, as Ralbag explains in *I Kings* 19:17, the figure of seven thousand reflects the survivors of Jehu, Chazael and Elisha, and many of the Baal worshippers may have died ear-

lier during the great famine, as described in *II Kings* 6:25.

27. Rashi, *I Kings* 20:13

28. *Metzudos David, II Kings* 8:26. The Prophet refers to her as Asaliah the daughter of Amri. *Metzudos* suggests that this may indicate that she was raised by her grandfather Amri. It is highly likely that this was indeed the case. Since according to Ralbag (*I Kings* 16:31), Jezebel was not converted to Judaism, her children were also not Jewish. Except for Yehoram, however, the kings of Israel would nonetheless be Jewish because of their Jewish mothers. But the problem arises with the kings of Judah. If Jezebel was not Jewish, then her daughter Asaliah was not Jewish either, and while the kings of Judah descended from her through her son Yoash would be considered Jewish because of their Jewish mothers, they would not be of Davidic descent. Therefore, we must assume that Asaliah was converted to Judaism, and her being raised by her grandfather Amri, who was not a Baal worshipper, would provide a reasonable explanation for her conversion. Otherwise, it is possible that Asaliah was the daughter of Ahab by another wife who was Jewish.

29. Bab. Tal., *Gittin* 88a refers to this evil dynasty as the House of Ahab, even though it was founded by his father Amri. Rashi explains that this is because Ahab was worse than his father.

30. *II Chronicles* 21:11

31. Rashi, *II Kings* 3:3

32. Bab. Tal., *Gittin* 88a

33. *II Kings* 18:21

34. Bab. Tal. *Sanhedrin* 110b

35. Rashi, *II Kings* 3:3

36. Bab. Tal., *Avos* 4:1

37. *II Chronicles* 31:1. However, as Malbim points out (*II Kings* 21:11), idolatry was not as widespread under Achaz as under his grandson Menasheh.

38. Bab. Tal., *Sanhedrin* 94a

39. *II Chronicles* 29:5-11

40. Bab. Tal., *Sanhedrin* 94b

41. *II Chronicles* 29:36; Rashi, *II Chronicles* 30:26

42. See Redak, *II Kings* 19:37

43. *The Histories*, Book Two

44. I. Velikovsky, *Ages in Chaos*

CHAPTER 7
EXILE AND RETURN

1. When the Prophet reports Menasheh's accession to the throne in *II Kings* 21:1, he identifies Menasheh's mother as Hepzebah. In general, the specific mention of a mother's name implies a measure of influence and responsibility (see *I Kings* 21:21,31 and *II Chronicles* 12:13 with regard to Rechavam and his mother Naamah). Therefore, the indication would seem to be that Hepzebah was, to some degree, responsible for Menasheh's crimes. However, *II Chronicles* 33:1 does not mention Hepzebah, which seems to indicate that her influence was not that great.

2. Bab. Tal., *Sanhedrin* 94a

3. Bab. Tal., *Sanhedrin* 90a

4. Malbim, *II Kings* 21:3

5. Bab. Tal., *Sanhedrin* 101b, 102b

6. *II Kings* 21:16, *Metzudos David.*

7. Bab. Tal., *Sanhedrin* 103b, *Yevamos* 49b

8. Rashi, *Isaiah* 1:1

9. Malbim, *II Kings* 21:11

10. Bab. Tal., *Sanhedrin* 103a

11. This episode appears in *II Chronicles* 33:11-17. It is omitted from *II Kings* because his repentance did not rectify the damage he had done. See Malbim, *II Kings* 21:15.

12. Rashi, *II Chronicles* 33:9

13. Bab. Tal., *Sanhedrin* 103b

14. Rashi, Malbim, *II Kings* 22:8

15. Deuteronomy 28:36-37

16. Rashi, *II Chronicles* 34:19

17. Rashi, Redak, *II Kings* 22:14. They also mention an alternate view that Chuldah was chosen because a woman, being more merciful, was

likely to be a more effective intercessor for the king.

18. Redak, *II Kings* 23:29
19. Redak, *II Kings* 23:33
20. Redak, *II Kings* 23:34
21. *Jeremiah* 7:3-7
22. *Jeremiah* 46:2; *II Kings* 24:7
23. The prophet does not mention a siege in the account of Nebuchadnezzar's conquest and arrest of Yehoakim, whereas the arrest of Yehoachin was preceded by a siege. Therefore, one can reasonably assume that Yehoachin fortified the city to resist attack. This is further supported by the brief duration of Yehoachin's reign. What had he done in those three months that prompted Nebuchadnezzar to lay siege to Jerusalem and remove him from the throne? Most probably, he had fortified the city against attack.
24. *II Kings* 24:19; *Jeremiah* 52:2; Bab. Tal., *Sanhedrin* 103a
25. *II Chronicles* 36:12; Bab. Tal., *Sanhedrin* 103a
26. *Ovadiah* 1:20
27. *Jeremiah* 52:11
28. Bab. Tal., *Arachin* 11b
29. The unbearable privations in the city during the siege, the frightful carnage that followed when the walls of the city were breached and the yearning of a people in exile are portrayed in excruciating detail in *The Book of Lamentations*, an eyewitness account by the prophet Jeremiah. This heartbreaking dirge is read in its entirety every year on the ninth day of the month of *Av*, an annual day of national mourning that is observed by the Jewish people to this very day.
30. *Jeremiah* 25:12
31. *Zechariah* 1:5
32. Bab. Tal., *Gittin* 88a
33. Tosefos, Bab. Tal., *Gittin* 6a
34. Bab. Tal., *Pesachim* 87b
35. Rashi, *Jeremiah* 52:30
36. Redak, *Jeremiah* 44:28
37. *Lamentations* 5:17-20
38. The correct Persian alliteration of this name is Chsharshya. In Hebrew, this guttural name is softened somewhat and becomes Achash-verosh. In Greek, with its paucity of harsh consonant sounds, the name is further adapted and becomes Xerxes. The Artaxerxes appears in Greek accounts as another of the Persian kings. This a Greek rendering of the name Artachshasta and an erroneous assumption. In actuality, this is a generic Persian term for king, such Pharaoh for the Egyptian kings and Avimelech for the Philistine kings. See Rashi, *Ezra* 4:7, 6:14.
39. Bab. Tal., *Megillah* 16b
40. See *Ezra* 7:7 and 7:24. Rashi, Bab. Tal., *Bava Basra* 8a, explains that this refers to the Men of the Great Assembly. Therefore, we can assume that the Assembly was already constituted in Babylon, although its most famous works were executed in Jerusalem.
41. See *II Kings* 3:15, wherein Elisha listens to the soothing strains of music in order to attain a state of mind capable of prophetic communication.
42. Meiri, Introduction to *Avos*
43. *Deuteronomy* 17:11
44. Bab. Tal., *Berachos* 19a
45. For example, the Solomonic regulations for the purposes of ritual purity, as mentioned in *Shabbos* 14b.
46. Bab. Tal., *Avos* 1:1
47. Bab. Tal., *Berachos* 33a
48. A full discussion of this restriction appears in Chapter 3.
49. Meiri, Introduction to *Avos*
50. Bab. Tal., *Avos* 1:1
51. Bab. Tal., *Sanhedrin* 102b
52. *Nehemiah* 9:4, explained by Bab. Tal., *Sanhedrin* 64a
53. *Ecclesiastes* 5:9, rephrased in *Koheles Rabbah* 1:34 as "whoever has a hundred wants two hundred"
54. Looking back from the vantage point of the distant future, we see a coincidence between the demise of the devotional impulse and the end

of prophecy. Perhaps we may even venture to surmise that there is a connection, that the removal of the devotional impulse somehow diminished the connection between man and God and hastened the end of the fading age of prophecy.

CHAPTER 8
THE RISE OF THE GREEKS

1. The Ionians were probably the original Greek tribe, and the other tribes were probably splinter groups that grew in size and eventually took on individual names, just as the major Canaanite splinter groups eventually took on individual names, as noted in Chapter 2.
2. Aristophanes, *Frogs*

CHAPTER NINE
FIRST ENCOUNTERS

1. *Metaphysics*
2. *Nicomachean Ethics*
3. The works of Aristotle offer a prime example. Students of philosophy still read and argue over Aristotle's *Ethics*. No biologist, however, would have any interest in reading Aristotle's *History of Animals*. Many of his conclusions have been disproved, and those that have survived are integrated into common knowledge, making Aristotle's biology a superfluous relic in which only historians may perhaps find some passing interest.
4. The term philosophy is used here in the general sense of subjective knowledge of the human condition and is meant to include similar studies, such as history according the modern analytical method, and creative pursuits such as literature and art.
5. Bab. Tal., *Yona* 69a
6. Josephus, *Antiquities*
7. According to *Doros Harishonim* (1:181, 195), Simon was not known as "the Just" during his own lifetime. He was known as Simon the son of Chonio, the High Priest. Simon had a grandson, however, who also became High Priest and bore the same name, Simon the son of Chonio. This second Simon was a rogue, and to distinguish between grandfather and grandson, people began referring to the first Simon posthumously as the *tzaddik*, "the one who was just."
8. Bab. Tal., *Avodah Zarah* 10a
9. Bab. Tal., *Sanhedrin* 91a